Youth Leadership in Sport and Physical Education

Youth Leadership in Sport and Physical Education

Tom Martinek and Don Hellison

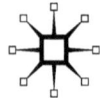

YOUTH LEADERSHIP IN SPORT AND PHYSICAL EDUCATION
Copyright © Tom Martinek and Don Hellison, 2009.
Softcover reprint of the hardcover 1st edition 2009 978-0-230-61236-5

All rights reserved.

First published in 2009 by
PALGRAVE MACMILLAN®
in the United States—a division of St. Martin's Press LLC,
175 Fifth Avenue, New York, NY 10010.

Where this book is distributed in the UK, Europe and the rest of the world, this is by Palgrave Macmillan, a division of Macmillan Publishers Limited, registered in England, company number 785998, of Houndmills, Basingstoke, Hampshire RG21 6XS.

Palgrave Macmillan is the global academic imprint of the above companies and has companies and representatives throughout the world.

Palgrave® and Macmillan® are registered trademarks in the United States, the United Kingdom, Europe and other countries.

ISBN 978-1-349-37720-6   ISBN 978-0-230-10132-6 (eBook)
DOI 10.1057/9780230101326

Library of Congress Cataloging-in-Publication Data

Martinek, Thomas J., 1943–
　　Youth leadership in sport and physical education / Tom Martinek and Don Hellison.
　　　p. cm.
　　Includes bibliographical references and index.

　　　1. Physical education and training—Sociological aspects. 2. Urban youth. 3. Leadership. I. Hellison, Donald R., 1938– II. Title.

GV342.27.M37 2009
613.7′043—dc22   2009017448

A catalogue record of the book is available from the British Library.

Design by Newgen Imaging Systems (P) Ltd., Chennai, India.

First edition: November 2009

10 9 8 7 6 5 4 3 2 1

Transferred to Digital Printing in 2011.

Contents

List of Figures	vii
List of Tables	ix
Foreword	xi
Preface	xiii
Acknowledgments	xix

Part I What's Worth Doing

1. Developing Youth into Leaders through Sport and Physical Education	3
2. Youth Development, Sport, and Youth Leadership	15
3. Youth Leadership, Social Justice, and Citizenship	27

Part II Stages of Youth Leadership

4. Stages of Youth Leadership Development	41
5. Stage One: Learning to Take Responsibility	51
6. Stage Two: Leadership Awareness	65
7. Stage Three: Cross-age Leadership	75
8. Stage Four: Self-actualized Leadership	89

Part III Making Leadership Work

9. Relationships with Leaders	103
10. Problem-solving in Youth Leadership	113
11. In-school Physical Education	125

Part IV Is It Working?

12. Assessment — 137
13. Research on Youth Leadership Programs — 153
14. Making It Happen — 165

Epilogue: Three Questions — 173
Appendix 1 — 179
References — 181
Index — 193

Figures

7.1	Give up the rock	84
8.1	Career path for the coaching club	93
12.1	Youth leader self-assessment rating form	140
12.2	Apprentice teacher self-evaluation form	141
12.3	Adult leader's assessment of leadership development	142
12.4	Trying in the classroom inventory	143
12.5	Program outcome model	148
12.6	Evaluation crosswalk	150

Tables

1.1	Personal and social responsibility levels	6
1.2	Club program format	6
4.1	Stages of leadership development	42
5.1	Levels of responsibility	53
6.1	Teaching cues for volleyball	68
6.2	Team practice plan	71
8.1	Career club workbook evaluation form	94
8.2	Internship journal card	97
9.1	Basic director–youth leader relationship qualities	104
9.2	Other director–youth leader relationship qualities	106
12.1	Adult-leader questionnaire	147

Foreword

Young people today, particularly those from underserved communities, are faced with numerous personal, social, economic, and academic challenges that leave many extremely vulnerable to multiple high-risk behaviors and school failures. With drug use, illegitimate births, violent crimes, and gang involvement among teenagers all on the rise, it is not surprising that youth development initiatives have become the major focus of many philanthropic organizations. What can be done? Well, one possibility is the widely held belief that positive sport experiences can help youth develop self-confidence and valuable life skills that enhance their capacity to handle the pressures and temptations that they face as teenagers today. Sport participation may also foster the leadership qualities that could enable young people to be active role models to others.

Nonetheless, based solely on the headlines of many sport pages today, one could easily ask the question, *does sport build character or does it create character disorders?* The easy answer to this complicated question is, *it depends.* So while most parents, recreation leaders, youth sport coaches, and physical educators espouse the value of sport and physical activity in teaching life skills to youth, research shows that none of the "lessons" learned on the playing field will transfer to the classroom or the boardroom unless youth are in the right context for growth.

For several decades, Tom Martinek and Don Hellison have modeled how to create the optimal context for fostering positive youth development. Imagine an environment that is fun, engaging, and challenging, but also one that has clear rules, requires personal responsibility, and demands that participants show respect for themselves and others. Imagine a process in which young people are treated with respect, empowered, and encouraged to excel. Imagine a learning strategy that is based on reflection and self-discovery. Now, imagine that all of this is happening with the support, encouragement, challenge that comes from having a quality relationship with caring adult mentors, and you begin to get a glimpse of why Tom and Don have been so instrumental in transforming the lives of countless, so called "at risk" youngsters.

On the basis of Don's Teaching Personal and Social Responsibility Model (TPSR), this book provides a wealth of information on how to develop and implement a leadership and life skills program for youth. You will not only learn the basics of TPSR, but you will also gain an understanding of how to overcome the various practical, logistical, and environmental challenges you are likely to face.

Beyond the knowledge and practical wisdom shared in this book, I hope that readers will be able to gain some insight into the humanism that characterizes Tom and Don, and their interactions with program participants. The new buzz word in positive youth development is *mattering*. The notion is that if young people believe that they matter, they will most likely invest the time and effort required to be successful in the selected activity and in life in general. Tom and Don help kids believe that they matter. People who are fortunate enough to interact with them undoubtedly walk away feeling understood, respected, and valued. Their positive and hopeful attitudes, and their genuine concern for the needs, well-being, and interests of their participants comes across in the quality of the relationships that they establish. After reading this book, I am confident that you will have a better understanding of how you can help young people believe that they really do *matter*.

AL PETITPAS
Springfield College

Preface: Youth Leadership through Sport and Physical Education

During our fifty years plus of working in school and community programs we have tried to better understand how character is shaped in children and youth who have been marginalized both socially and economically. Armed with a common set of responsibility values, we have used physical activity to help kids take responsibility for their own well being and the well-being of others. The genesis of our approach to leadership development originates from the second author's (Don) Teaching Personal and Social Responsibility (TPSR) model (Hellison, 1995, 2003). TPSR through physical activity is based on strong instructor-participant relationships. These relationships are closely tied to a specific set of guidelines, eventual power-sharing, and individual and group reflection. The model provides a set of values that can be fostered through designed physical activity experiences. One of these values, *leading and helping others* (Hellison, 2003, pp. 33–34) provided a jumping off point for writing this book.

Our youth development work, which continues today, has given us ample moments of discovery about the capabilities and fallibilies of underserved youth (i.e., at-risk, troubled, drop-out bound kids). We have written, recalled, and shared with others the things we see, hear, and feel. From the very moment kids walk through the gym doorway we have tried to capture bits and pieces of evidence that help us do better work and improve it as we reflect on it. But what have really grabbed our attention are those moments, even the fleeting ones that unveil the capacity of adolescent youth to impact the lives of others.

For us, seeing kids lead and help others elevates resilience (i.e., the ability to bounce) to another level. The importance of all this is to recognize that youth leadership development furthers the acquisition of positive healthy and risk reducing behaviors. In other words, when young people serve as leaders—good things happen. Risk factors are reduced and protective factors such as social competence and confidence emerge.

That's why leadership development should be an important consideration of any program or organization that is serving adolescents.

Youth Leadership in Sport and Physical Education is for adult leaders who want to pursue similar goals in youth development programming. The term "adult leaders" refers to individuals who work with youths in recreation programs, YMCAs, YWCAs, Boys and Girls Clubs, church programs, and various after-school enrichment programs. Adult leaders also include teachers and/or coaches in school physical education or athletic programs, and university faculty. We recognize that the contexts in which adult leaders work are quite different from one another. Consequently, we present our ideas about youth leadership development in ways that can be used in a variety of settings. We also wanted the words and ideas of this book to relate directly to you. In other words, we want you to be in the same room with us. To do this we use the "the first person" (e.g., "you" and "we") throughout most of the book.

Although we will address you the reader as if you are interested in starting a sport-based leadership program, we realize that people may pick up this book for a variety of reasons, not all of which involve professional development. Some of you may be teachers, coaches, or youth workers, but others may be university professors interested in sharing this information with your students and still others may just be interested in learning more about using sport to teach leadership. So if you are not directly involved with kids who may gain from having a leadership program, don't stop reading because our writing style assumes that you are. Just ignore the "in your program" wording and read on.

More importantly, this is a book for those who view *all* kids as potential leaders and helpers. It is a book for those who see leadership as a way of promoting positive attitudes and respect as it is about achieving success. And, it is a book for those who envision leadership as a way of *serving* the needs of others, *changing* the setting where leadership is prioritized, and *making a moral difference* in the lives of others.

Our years of work with underserved kids and professionals who serve them have given us ideas about what works best with most kids. These ideas are just *ideas*... nothing more. They are presented for you in a still-evolving developmental framework. The framework is designed to help stimulate action for program development as well as continual self-reflection and evaluation.

At the same time, we are aware of the multitude of legitimate ways of understanding and teaching youth leadership. More specifically, various leaders design different programs using different models and pedagogies. For example, there is Charlie Tribe's (2008) youth leadership program, *Sports 37*, where training for Chicago's inner-city youths is provided so they can teach and coach younger kids in the Park District's summer sport programs. Kids also get certified to, for example, referee youth soccer games or be a lifeguard which turn into paid positions during the summer.

In New Zealand, Murray Turner (2007), has developed a specialized leadership program in his high school physical education classes. A leadership project is assigned to each student so they can independently experience what its like to *develop and lead* a specific program for kids.

Another leadership program headed by Aaron Dworkin (Berlin et al., 2007) is called the Hoops and Leader Basketball Camp. By leveraging the game of basketball, New York City's urban youth are taught leadership skills through careful mentoring and exposed to different educational and career opportunities. Finally, there is the Project Coach Program (Intractor & Siegel, 2008) that utilizes the resources of a college and four core youth development concepts to provide a cross-age leadership sports program for underserved kids.

While the above examples illustrate a variety of ways by which youth leadership programs function, two important qualities need to be present for any program to take hold (Klau, Boyd, & Luckow, 2006). First, the program plan must be clear about the model of leadership (set of values) it holds at its core. Adult leaders often speak of leadership as a program outcome, but do not have a conceptualization of leadership nor a process for this to occur.

Second, adult leaders must insure that the core model of leadership is aligned with the pedagogies used to teach it. In other words, the teaching strategies and values of the model must be integrated rather than taught separately.

We provide real life examples to clarify the various ideas for starting and maintaining a youth leadership program. The book is divided into four main parts. The first part, *What's Worth Doing*, includes three chapters. The first chapter emphasizes the importance of having adolescents viewed as leaders. We describe our view of leadership including basic assumptions that underlie leadership development. Our own personal histories of youth development are also profiled so you will get a sense of where our ideas and values come from.

The second chapter describes the field of youth development and its relationship to professional development, sport, and youth leadership. The emergence of youth development as a close affiliate of professional practice is underscored in this chapter. Thus, sport activities for developing leadership skills in youth become especially relevant.

The third chapter illustrates how the spirit of social justice and citizenship become intertwined in responsibility-based youth leadership programming. The use of TPSR values is foundational in upholding the right of young people to experience and apply the concepts of power sharing, inclusion, fairness, and other basic human rights. Examples of how youth have been advocates for social justice and active participants in small and large types of social reform are cited in this chapter.

Chapters 4, 5, 6, 7, and 8 make up the second part of the book: *Stages of Youth Leadership*. An overview of developmental stages of leadership is presented in the fourth chapter. The stages of leadership development are introduced as a way of viewing and assessing progression. They are: Stage One: Learning to Take Responsibility, Stage Two: Leadership Awareness, Stage Three: Cross-age Leadership, and Stage Four: Self-actualized Leadership. Basic requirements called "themes" are also offered. The themes are the ingredients for insuring the adolescent's advancement through the stages of development. The themes, *power-sharing*, *self- reflection*, *relationships*, *transfer,* and *integration* help to maintain consistency across the leadership experiences.[1] That is, they should be threaded through your leadership program. The specific stages of leadership development are then described in each of the following four chapters. Strategies for enhancing leadership within each stage are described with examples of how they work.

Chapters 9, 10, and 11 make up the third part, *Making Leadership Work*. Developing relationships between you and the youth leaders is essential to all that you attempt within each stage of development. Of the five themes earlier listed, the relationship one is the most important. That is why we devote an entire chapter to it (chapter 9). No matter what the intent of your leadership programming is, failing to connect to the leaders and all those with whom you work will render your program mediocre at best!

Our chapter 10 describes ways to problem solve through the challenges that lie ahead in programming planning and implementation. These challenges vary according to context, support, and feelings of uncertainty. Consequently, knowing how to address each one given your circumstance will be vital for success.

The eleventh chapter broadens the context in which youth leadership programs can take place. This chapter specifically focuses on in-school leadership programs. Both national and international school programs are described. Issues facing physical education programs in promoting youth leadership qualities are presented. School size and program goals, that is, TPSR values, are also considered in school-based programming.

Chapters 12, 13, 14, and epilogue make up the last part of the book: *Is It Working?* In chapter 12 we give examples of ways to assess your leadership programs. We have found that there is no single approach to evaluating the dynamics of leadership development. Some ways work better than others and both of us are fully aware that evaluating youth leader programs will be done with "cautious" interpretation.

Chapter 13 explores the studies that have examined various aspects of TPSR sport and leadership programs. Multiple data sources and methods are described with each serving its own purpose for examining nuances and impact of leadership programming.

The fourteenth chapter and epilogue will help you get started and help you reflect on your readiness to begin your own leadership program. Both will provide thoughts about the personal requirements needed to organize and implement the type of leadership program we have talked about throughout the book.

Our hope is that this book will further heighten your interest and will to help youth become key players to community enrichment and goodwill. Whether you are a teacher, coach, counselor, and someone who works in youth agencies, you will acquire a sense of purpose from reading this book. That purpose is to help youth discover the wonderful legacies they can leave at the doorstep of their families, school, and communities. Our intent is to equip you with a set of ideas that will help you guide young people through this journey of discovery. In the end helping them develop their leadership potential helps us all.

Tom & Don

Note

1. Four of the five themes have been borrowed from Hellison's *Teaching responsibility through physical activity*. They are both appropriate and useful in helping to architect strategies for moving adolescents along the three stages of leadership development.

Acknowledgments

A nice thing about writing this book is that it reminds us of the many individuals who have given us ideas, support, guidance, and inspiration for doing this work. We are incredibly grateful to all of them for not only being a huge part of this book, but of our lives.

We begin by giving thanks to all the kids with whom we have worked, sweated, cried, and rejoiced over the past years. When anyone asks us "What truly inspires you to do this work?" our response has always been "because it is the right thing to do." There is irony to all this. By helping them gain purpose and meaning in their lives, we have benefitted the same way in ours. We will always be grateful for that gift.

We also want to give thanks to past principal and vice principal, Penny Kerr and Paul Butler of Chicago's Bond School and the Deborah Jones principal of Greensboro's Hampton Elementary School. If it were not for them our programs would never have been launched. Equally important, is the wonderful work of past graduate students, *Nick Cutforth*, *Nikos Georgiadis*, *Dave Walsh*, *Dennis Johnson*, *Dan McLaughlin*, *Tammy Schilling*, and *Paul Wright*. All of them are now at other universities creating their own programs, helping kids, or simply, carrying the torch.

I

What's Worth Doing

1
Developing Youth into Leaders through Sport and Physical Education

Bloom where you are planted.

—Nancy Reader Campion

During our work with the Teaching Personal and Social Responsibility (TPSR) model in school and community sport programs we constantly see evidence of how young people can become leaders in large and small ways. We have come to believe *all* adolescents have leadership potential when given opportunity and guidance. This belief is bolstered by a wider vision of leadership that reaches beyond the traditional "top-down" view held by many. Personal and social responsibility with a particular focus on caring and compassion for others become the cornerstones of the type of leadership we are talking about. Inspired by Walter Percy's phrase "we hand one another along" (Coles, 2000) we further see our approach to leadership as having an important pay back. It is capable of empowering others to be leaders in their own community (e.g., neighborhood, home, schools, recreation centers, churches, etc.). Involvement in a school's service learning project, volunteering for a community enrichment project, coaching a youth sport team, helping out at a local Boys and Girls Club, or simply being a good parent are just a few of the ways by which this pay back can be realized.

While our kids have assumed some leadership roles, those they have taken are often negative ones (i.e., bullying others, leading in a gang, controlling classroom climate). This is because these same kids have had few, if any, opportunities to act as positive leaders during their lifetime. This lack of opportunities is especially true in their schools.

Positive leadership is only offered to a few select students because of their popularity and/or certain personal attributes (i.e., inspirational, organized, intelligent, charismatic, assertive, confident). In other words, most schools seem to draw the line rather than open up possibilities for our kids, thus making their vision of leadership quite limited. In fact, many teachers and administrators insist that they are inherently incompetent and irresponsible. Former New York City's Bard College president Leon Botstein (Epstein, 2007) (and both of us) think differently. He contends that teens can be more capable than many adults in assuming higher levels of responsibility (i.e., leadership roles). In actuality, he argues that even the neediest young person requires more responsibility, not less!

Our View of Youth Leadership

The question is, then, how can *all* adolescents be helped to become aware of their leadership skills? Kouzes and Pouzner (1987) claim that opportunities to lead can be categorized in three ways: trial and error, people, and education. *Trial and error* means learning by doing. Being a school club officer, captain of a team, or an active participant in a community service program are examples of positions in which youngsters can learn by doing. *People* can also be instrumental in forming leadership skills. Coaches, teachers, counselors, and parents provide feedback and guidance in the learning process. They also become role models.

Structured *leadership education* represents the third way to learn about being a leader. Our approach is a combination of all three. While some structure is necessary, there needs to be room for trying out new ideas as well as positive role modeling by adult leaders.

One of our goals for this book is to present an alternative conception of leadership that includes *helping others* as one of its priorities. The youth leaders we are talking about are those who displace urges of self-indulgence with spirited service to others. Our approach to leadership, therefore, links responsibility and service to others as its cornerstones (Libby, Sedonaen, & Bliss, 2006). For us, it is the type of leadership that helps others confront the social and physical challenges found in neighborhood sport clubs, homes, soup kitchens, athletic fields, churches, and, yes, even schools.

We also are fully aware of the many challenges kids face in becoming caring and compassionate leaders. Youngsters who confront social and economic neglect and an educational system that marginalizes them in many ways find it especially difficult. Therefore, another major goal we have is to show how you can equip youngsters with a set of skills and attitudes that can be learned and practiced in a variety of life situations. By reading this book, you will have, at hand, a set of ideas that can enable you to help adolescents arrive at the realization that they can truly impact the lives of others. But the ideas themselves will not automatically transform kids into leaders. Rather, their successful application will be dependent on the degree to which you embrace a broader inclusive view of leadership as well as your relational and teaching skills.

Sources of Our Ideas

Where do our ideas come from? Many of them come from our values as well as personal experiences and related insights as teachers in youth sport programs. Over the years these programs have provided values-based instruction for hundreds of underserved children and youth.

One program headed by Tom operates at the University of North Carolina at Greensboro (UNCG). The other is headed by Don at the University of Illinois at Chicago (UIC). The program at UNCG is called the Youth Leader Corps program and has been operating for ten years. The one at UIC is called the Urban Youth Leader Project and has been running for seventeen years. Both programs provide opportunities for participants to develop leadership skills by teaching sport and life skills to younger kids from various community agencies and programs (e.g., Boys and Girls Club, Head Start, National Youth Sport Program). Many youth leaders attend one of the local schools, while some are either in alternative schools or pursuing a Graduate Education Development Certificate (GED). And, there are a few who have dropped out of school because of pregnancy or incarceration, but still attend (or come back to) the leadership programs.

All our youth leaders have previously participated in a sport club, not as leaders but as participants (i.e., club members). The "club" concept is emphasized at all times to the students so they feel that they have "ownership" in the program. Don's has two clubs called the "Coaching Club" and "Martial Arts Leadership Club." Tom's is called "Project Effort Sport Club." All clubs allow students to participate in physical activity experiences that foster personal and social responsibility. The club experiences also wean kids into more responsible leadership roles—something that will be addressed later in this book.

Our clubs are based on the goals of teaching personal and social responsibility through physical activity shown in table 1.1. The five student goals listed in table 1.1 are a loose progression of responsibilities that lead up to the goal of helping and leading others. To truly be a leader-as-role-model, students must first be able to respect the rights and feelings of others, cooperate and show effort, and engage in self-directed activities such as goal-setting. Instructional processes necessary to facilitate goal attainment include gradual power-sharing, group- and self-reflection, and most importantly, the development of positive and supportive relationships with each student.

Table 1.1 Personal and social responsibility levels

Level One:	Respecting for the rights and feelings of others	
	• Self-control	
	• The right to peaceful resolution	
	• The right to be included	
Level Two:	Participation and effort	
	• Self-motivation	
	• Exploration of effort and new tasks	
	• Courage to persist when the going gets tough	
Level Three:	Self-direction	
	• On-task independence	
	• Goal-setting progression	
	• Courage to resist peer pressure	
Level Four:	Helping and leading others	
	• Caring and compassion	
	• Sensitivity and responsiveness	
	• Inner strength	
Level Five:	Outside the gym	
	• Trying the above levels in others areas of life	
	• Being a role model	

Table 1.2 Club program format

Part of Lesson	What goes on
1. Relational time:	Counseling and relational time while kids work on their own or with another club member
2. Awareness talk:	Awareness talk to open lesson. Teacher reminds students of their goals with student participation
3. Physical activity lesson:	Teacher integrates student goals into the lesson & problem-solves as needed
4. Group meeting:	Teacher listens to students' positive & negative comments about the lesson, as well as suggestions to improve the lesson
5. Self-reflection time:	Students self-evaluate how well they carried out their goals, including "Outside the gym"

A program format, shown in table 1.2, builds these processes into the daily program. Implementing these goals, processes, and format gradually creates a unique climate where students can "let their guard down," explore new activities and experiences, and learn to relate positively to each other.

Youth Leadership Issues

According to Klau and his associates (Klau, Boyd, & Luckow, 2006), youth leadership in youth development "remains largely unexplored" (p. 3), despite the growing number of programs that claim to teach youth leadership. They suggest several issues that need to be addressed to advance the development of youth leadership. Our lengthy experiences with youth leadership have shaped our responses to these issues, and are shown in italics following each of the issues:

- The relation of youth leadership to social justice (see chapter 3). *Our goal is to help kids become caring and compassionate leaders which, at its best, promotes a climate of equity, fairness, and support for those who need an extra boost.*
- "Inside versus outside leadership" (p. 4). *We focus on developing leaders inside our youth programs with a specific goal of transfer to other settings.*
- Leadership that designates an authority versus leadership for everyone, and its corollary, leadership for all versus leadership for the select few. *Our version of leadership can be acquired by all.*
- Youth as future leaders versus youth as leaders now. *We begin work on kids becoming leaders when kids first walk in the door (as early as fourth grade).*
- "The challenge of youth-adult partnerships in leadership education" (p. 5). *We view all youth work as primarily relational. Without strong relationships with youth, nothing works well.*
- What model of youth leadership promotes a sense of community, and do instructional strategies reflect this model? *These last two questions are at the heart of this book, so read on!*

Why We Believe It's Important to Develop Kids as Leaders

We decided to write this book for one simple reason. We wanted to explain to others our philosophy and practices of working with adolescent youth and we wanted to do this in a way that readers could understand how to encourage youth to view themselves as resources for others and their community. Schools, and even some well-intended community programs, often sidestep opportunities to provide *all kids* those opportunities to be socially responsible for the welfare and development of others.

For adolescent underserved youth, this lack of leadership development is an especially critical omission. Most are on a "cultural shopping trip" trying to figure where they belong within the mainstream of school. Diane Ackerman (1996) reminds us that for underserved kids there is a "slender thread" between kids' realization and loss of self-worth. Our ideas in this book attempt to help adult program leaders alter adolescents' perspective. That is, replacing their tunnel vision with a more expanded view of their strengths. The inclusion of leadership experiences can create more social space (Halpern, 2003) to explore and discover those assets that will eventually benefit others and the community.

The Role of Physical Activity in Leadership Development

Youth leadership programs have gained national attention in recent years. In fact, a recent issue of *New Directions for Youth Development* was devoted to the topic (Klau, Boyd, & Luckow, 2006). Leadership programs have been inherently multifaceted and complex employing different models and pedagogies. Many of the pedagogies include activities such as workbook exercises, group discussion, role playing, and group problem solving. Although these experiences have merit, few, if any, exploit physical activity as means for teaching leadership skills.

We see physical activity-based programs as having enormous potential in creating leadership skills. One reason for this is that physical activity is highly interactive. Its context creates many "natural" opportunities for youth to explore both one-and-one and group-lead leadership exploration. Physical activity also challenges young leaders to respond to spontaneous circumstances that may arise. In a basketball game, for example, these "leadership moments" might require defusing an argument over a call, enforcing certain rules for his or her team members (e.g., no trash talk), or making sure that no one is excluded from touching the ball. And, many of these "moments" can ignite moral introspection and action by the youth leader. They provide ample opportunity to bring together the moral meaning of that moment during a game and experiences of life itself.

Finally, physical activity is something that kids enjoy whether they are participants in a club or leaders. Barton Hirsch's (2005) research of over 300 youth club participants clearly underscores the alluring qualities that physical activity has for kids. Comparative data (with games, club programs, computers, artistic activities) showed that physical activities were the "overwhelming reason" for coming to the club settings. Thus, physical activity creates a "comfort zone" which better enables them to meet the demands of being a leader. However, our approach goes beyond Hirsch's use of physical activity as a hook to entice kids into the program. As stated above we are interested in embedding youth leadership principles in physical activity content.

Fortunately, the youth development movement is beginning to acknowledge the role of sport as a vehicle for teaching youth development principles, as a recent issue of *New Directions for Youth Development* titled "*Sports-based Youth Development*" (Perkins & Menestrel, 2007) attests (see chapter 2). The emergence of sport leadership programs cited in our preface (e.g., Berlin et al., 2007; Intractor & Siegel, 2008; Tribe, 2008; Turner, 2007) further strengthens the case for sport-based youth development programs.

Challenges in Becoming Leaders

The TPSR model (see table 1.1) that has guided our physical activity programs (a.k.a. Sport & Coaching Clubs) has a fourth level—helping and leading others This level represents a critical threshold for becoming socially responsible. Our work (Martinek, Schilling, & Hellison, 2006, Hellison & Martinek, 2006a) suggests that adolescents do not all of a sudden become leaders. Rather they go through what Jerome Burns (1978) calls a transformational process where sensitivity to the needs and values of others begins to grow. That is, youth leaders acquire a sense of responsibility to self and others.

Helping others (especially in a compassionate and caring way) has many challenges for an adolescent. One challenge is to rebuff peer pressure; helping another in a caring and compassionate way is not always cool! The norms and values of one's own peer group and the media make it difficult to shed the value of "being tough" for the sake of helping someone out. Believing that young people have the potential for being responsible individuals will be important for helping kids meet this challenge.

Another challenge is not to lead others with an air of superiority. Many kids feel that leading others is a chance to have control over others. After all, this is what they see daily from their teachers, coaches, club leaders, and parents! Unfortunately, such images of power are prevalent and rewarded in our society. Since having a sense of control is so vital to our kids, it is little wonder as to why many choose to lead with arrogance and, sometimes, intimidation.

The third challenge is for adolescents to become intrinsically motivated to help others. Some students take on the leadership role because they want to please us (adult leaders) or receive some extrinsic reward (e.g., money, food). That's why stressing responsibility level four is so important. Being compassionate and caring leaders must be intrinsically motivated—coming from one's heart. Only those leaders who are sensitive to someone else's needs can then be responsive to them (Hellison, 2003). We have found that students who are extrinsically motivated will eventually slack off and/or lose the meaning of level four.

Personal life events represent a final challenge for leaders. Many of our leaders have experienced the pain of having family members and/or friends lost to street violence. Some have been personally victimized by abandonment, physical and sexual abuse, pregnancy, and incarceration. These extreme life events create a circuitous pathway toward their development as leaders. But despite all their "ups" and "downs" we are often amazed by those who are willing to show up and work with other kids. The persistence of those who are able to leave "street issues" outside the gym door reminds us of their incredible humanity and desire to help others.

Leadership Programming—Is This for Me?

Teaching young people to be caring and compassionate leaders will require more than mere interest. Obstacles and self doubt will creep in when pushing kids to assume leadership roles. New capacities will be needed. Special conditions for programs and youth-adult and youth-youth interactions will be needed. The remainder of this book provides details.

When we started our leadership programs we confronted daunting questions. For example:

- could we personally deal with kids who didn't show up?
- could we cope with the leaders' good and bad days?
- how much nudging would it take to get certain kids to step up?

- how far do you go with a leader's indifference and lack of responsibility to the leadership role...that is, when do you tell him or her that it's time to go?

Quincy Howe, who taught in a residential center for abandoned youth, claims that cultivating purpose in kids requires a careful examination of one's own human qualities (Howe, 1991). By critically examining our values, beliefs, and commitment we found that we could better confront the challenges that hinder progress in our work. Therefore, careful examination of your personal values is a must before trying to get adolescent youth to become caring and compassionate leaders. An important first step in creating a leadership program like the one we will be presenting in this book is to first examine your own values about working with kids. Here are three important beliefs about kids that you need to have before starting.

Kids are capable of leading. If we assume that only certain students can be leaders, that is, we believe that *leaders are born, not made*, there is little use for a leadership programming. At the same time, we know kids will vary in their underlying values about helping others—life experiences will do that. Some will have a sense of helping others because it is the right thing to do. Others may eventually readjust their negative attitudes if given the leadership experience with feedback and counseling as necessary. Thus, believing that all kids are capable of leading others becomes an integral quality of the TPSR model. Besides values, an individual kid's *relational skills* either hamper or facilitate the leadership process. All are capable, but some enter the program with more of the needed skills than others.

Both of us have seen numerous examples of youth leadership in our programs. When leadership is viewed this way then individuals are freed up to discover their gifts, talents, and skills that can guide them to become successful leaders (Hellison et al., 2000). Unfortunately, society is fixated on highlighting the inadequacies of today's youth. You must think differently! Taking on the responsibility of developing young leaders will then require you to see beyond the headlines and see young people as potential leaders for your program.

Kids can be caring people. Robert Coles (1998) contends that caring and compassion for others is a natural and important part of children's lives from the time of their first relationships. Studies by Ackerman and colleagues show true friendships taking shape between the ages of one and three years (Eckerman, Davis, & Didow, 1989; Eckerman & Didow, 1988). For many, the drive to help others comes from a need to be accepted. Noted child psychologist Judith Harris (1998) proposes that young children are very connected to their playmates, much more so than they are to their parents. They place great value on being able to imitate, lead, and follow others so they can be connected to "the group."

It is also true that some kids, young and old, can be selfish, unfeeling, and just plain mean. They can be harmful to others as much as they can be helpful (Damon, 1990). Negative "street values," the glamorization of violence in the media, and the endearment of a "me" culture by entertainment and sport figures are often the main culprits here and will not disappear. Therefore, if you are to nurture the "caring instinct" in adolescents you have to feel that youth leadership development is worth doing and approach your kids positively, but not naively.

Kids are capable decision-makers. In later chapters we address the concept of empowerment—a key concept of the responsibility model. In order to empower kids one has to believe that they are capable decision-makers; they can effectively take on the responsibilities of their leadership roles: planning, teaching, and evaluating. The research on youth programs (see Benson, 2006, Hellison & Cutforth, 1997; McLaughlin & Heath, 1993) clearly indicate that programs having the most impact are ones that allow youth to make choices. Adult guidance is imperative when giving choices since most youth are not used to having the responsibility of making decisions that will benefit them. According to Katherine Kress (2006), our culture places youth in powerless situations with no meaningful role other than consumers. She further points out (p. 51): "…many adults [program leaders] do not understand that their role is not to mold participants in their programs but to provide tools and opportunities for youth to discover their unique spirit, genius, and public life." Responsibility and empowerment go hand-in-hand. And they are not about compliance to arbitrary standards. Rather, empowering youth to be autonomous leaders significantly widens the capability to gain a sense of control over their lives.

Now that you are ready for this great adventure in leadership programming, you will need to read on! As a "jumping-off point" for the rest of the book the next two chapters will situate youth leadership development within the broader contexts of youth development, sport, social justice, and citizenship. All four play critical roles in our understanding and application of best practices for fostering positive and healthy youth leadership development. Recognizing their relationship to leadership development will help to form the basis for purpose and goal enhancement of your leadership program.

Insights and Take-aways

The following are the some of the main points of this chapter for you to remember:

- The Teaching Social and Personal Responsibility Model (TPSR) is used as a guide to form experiences that *lead up* to the goal of helping and leading others.
- Important issues have been largely unexplored and need to be addressed in order to advance the development of youth leadership. They are as follows: (a) the relation of youth leadership to social justice, (b) inside versus outside leadership, (c) leadership by authority versus leadership for everyone, (d) youth and future leaders versus youth as leaders now, (e) the challenge of youth-adult partnerships, and (f) identifying a model of youth leadership promotes a sense of community.
- Physical activity has enormous potential in creating leadership skills in adolescents. It's highly interactive, provides natural situations for one-on-one and group-lead exploration, and is inherently enjoyable for kids.
- Teaching kids to be caring and compassionate leaders requires careful introspection. Thee important beliefs about kids are important to have: (a) kids are capable of leading, (b) kids can be caring people, and (c) kids are capable decision-makers.

2
Youth Development, Sport, and Youth Leadership

The club is helping me because before I was in it I had a very bad attitude.

—*Coaching Club member*

Professional preparation and in-service training for coaches, physical education teachers, youth workers, and other physical activity program leaders are key factors in the development of quality youth programs. Historically, professional preparation has been uneven and sometimes nonexistent. Moreover, it has paid less attention to, or even neglected altogether, the potential link between physical activity and life skills/values development, despite the rampant "sport builds character" rhetoric. The recent emergence of the field of youth development offers hope for a shift in professional preparation and eventually the quality of youth programs toward educating youth more holistically. The advent of youth development has been of particular interest to us, because youth development strongly promotes youth empowerment and leadership, just as we have tried to do for many years. Unfortunately, it took a while for the physical activity field to see the relevance of youth development for physical activity programs for kids, but this is now changing. The result is more support for the development of holistic youth leadership through sport, physical education, and other physical activities.

Professional Preparation for Sport and Physical Education

Professional development opportunities for physical activity practitioners currently include:

- Physical education teacher education certification programs.
- Optional or minimal coach education programs for school sport and youth sport coaches.
- Instructional certification programs other than teacher certification for fitness instructors, aquatics professionals, and some sports such as soccer.
- Occasional professional development workshops for youth workers and others conducted mostly by outside consultants.

The quality of professional preparation varies widely, including no training at all, for example, in some sport-based programs in community organizations.

Historically, mandated certification programs for school coaches have been limited and often minimal, while youth sport coach education programs outside of schools have been at least to some extent costly, time-consuming, and therefore not very appealing to volunteer coaches. The National Association of Sport and Physical Education developed national standards for sport coaches, and 84 percent of states have some kind of a coaching education requirement. However, the states differ markedly regarding who must meet the requirement, who governs the program, and what content is required. Recently, the advent of online education has attracted many more coaches and as a result significantly expanded coach education in schools and youth sport. The National Federation of High Schools now offers an online certification program (http://www.nfhslearn.com), and the online program of Craig Stewart at Montana State University averages 4,000 participants a year in Montana alone (http://www.coacheducation.org/php/coaching.php). His program, based on National Association of Sport and Physical Education guidelines, is also used as a coaching minor at Montana State University. The cost of these online programs is minimal, and that in addition to the accessibility accounts for the rise in certified coaches. Currently, youth sport coaches actually surpass interscholastic sport coaches in accessing these programs.

In-service workshops are sometimes offered to teachers, coaches, and youth workers, but consultants rarely donate their time, so someone has to provide workshop funding. Moreover, typical "one shot" workshops (i.e., one session without follow-up) are not very effective in promoting professional development.

Community- and faith-based organizations often offer a wide variety of physical activity programs for kids—from "open gym" to sport and exercise clubs and programs devoted to adventure and outdoor activities, jazz dance, hip hop, tumbling, self-defense, martial arts, and the usual team and individual sports. However, the professional qualifications of youth leaders in these organizations vary widely as does program oversight.

The Emergence of Youth Development

Youth development, a new "player" on the youth work scene in recent years, has begun to nudge these trends in professional training for physical activity professionals, especially in the content delivered in teacher training, coach education programs, and workshops, but also to some extent in broadening professional preparation opportunities.

In the United States, the field of youth development emerged slowly from the days of Jane Addams' work in Chicago (Addams, 1909) to what it is today. Halpern (2003) pegged the 1990's as time that youth development really became a force in community-based programs. In that same time period, Dewitt-Wallace Reader's Digest Fund supported *Strengthening the youth work profession* (1996), a five million dollar study of inner city after-school youth programs spurred by after-school violence and the need for more youth guidance. Most of the funding went to the Academy for Educational Development's Center for Youth Development and Public Policy to support an investigation of urban programs across the country. The Center's findings included a wide range of weaknesses in the programs studied, from program content to the professional preparation of staff.

As a result, "The Academy" held a conference and achieved consensus on a definition of a new field of participants called youth development, including a conceptualization of key youth development principles. These findings—which included the development of personal, social, and citizenship competencies with a focus on empowerment and responsibility—were circulated to community organizations across the country (*Strengthening the youth work profession*, 1996) and probably marked the beginning of widespread use of the term youth development, sometimes with little understanding of its meaning.

Others were responsible for further developing youth development as a field and as a perspective. Peter Benson's assortment of internal and external assets (1997) was influential in raising youth workers' awareness of asset-based rather than deficit-based goals and processes. The term assets began to appear in mission statements, workshops, and the youth work literature. Another force, the academically powerful National Research Council (2002), led by a select group of youth development academics and professionals, provided the beginning of a research base for youth development, including the promotion of evidence-based studies of effective program designs, implementation plans, and evaluation techniques.

These highlights in the shift to a youth development perspective were joined by the work of others as well, notably Psychologist Richard Lerner's (2004) theoretical-based approach to youth development practices and policies and the practice-based work of Milbrey McLaughlin and her associates (McLaughlin, Irby, & Langman, 1994; McLaughlin, 2000). Among other things, McLaughlin's work in combination with the thinking of other youth work professionals resulted in eleven key youth development criteria for after-school programs in underserved communities (Hellison & Cutforth, 1997). Highlights included a general characterization of good programs as being holistic and developmental. This characterization included aspects like having a caring adult leader, an emotionally as well as physically safe environment, and small numbers of kids who belong to a club or team, and participate regularly over multiple years. McLaughlin's point about the importance of a caring adult has been made by others as well (Rhodes, 2004; Seligson & Stahl, 2003). The embedded curriculum (Hamilton & Hamilton, 2004)—which refers to embedding youth development principles in art, music, sport, and other youth program content—also emerged during this nascent period of growth.

Accompanying this rapid growth of youth development ideas and processes has been a spate of new journals and newsletters (e.g., *Youth today, New Directions for Youth Development: Theory, Practice, and Research*), books and articles (see references at the end of this chapter), organizations (e.g., National Network for youth, National Youth Leadership Council, Forum for Youth Investment), and academic programs of study (e.g., University of Minnesota, University of Illinois at Chicago). Centers and institutes are also popping up here and there (the Harvard Program in After-school Education and Research, the Applied Developmental Science Institute at Tufts University). As is often the case, the practice of youth development has lagged behind these fast-paced conceptual and philosophical changes, although a number of exemplary youth development programs have been cited in the burgeoning literature.

The upshot of all this activity to promote holistic development among today's youth has been a wide range of overlapping but sometimes confusing guidelines (e.g., Benson, 1997; Noam, Biancarosa, & Dechausay, 2003; Brendtro, Brokenleg, & Van Bockern, 2005) but fewer evidence-based studies (the National Research Council, 2002). Such is the state of a young field.

Sport-based Youth Development

Although physical activity programs are very popular in after-school and summer programs, the new field of youth development was slow to view sport as a true youth development activity. Instead, it was viewed mostly as a "hook," a way to attract kids to the program rather than a vehicle for embedding youth development principles (Hartmann, 2003; Hirsch, 2005). Physical activity practitioners and scholars were culpable as well, showing little enthusiasm for the contribution of youth development to physical activity programs for children and youth. Park and recreation leaders, on the other hand, were quick to see its relevance and began to adopt and promulgate youth development principles (Witt & Crompton, 2002).

Physical education has a rich history of arguing for "education through the physical" to capitalize on the highly active, interactive, and emotional nature of many physical activities (Siedentop, 1990). Youth development concepts such as empowerment and leadership easily could be embedded in the physical activity content to promote holistic development. However, while the early advocacy of education through the physical did alter the rhetoric of many sport and physical education leaders, practices in these programs in gyms and on playing fields remained quite traditional for the most part.

Recent signs of change suggest if not a major shift in the field at least a little elbow room for youth development-inclined professionals to operate. Sport psychologist Al Petitpas, one of the early and still very active leaders in the field, has been instrumental in developing and promoting two national sport-based youth development programs, First Tee and Play it Smart (Petitpas, Cornelius, & Van Raalte, 2008). He and his associates have also made several other important contributions to the literature, including a framework of four different types of sport-based youth development programs (Petitpas et al., 2005). His Youth Development through Sport Center at Springfield College was one of the first centers or institutes in higher education devoted to sport-based youth development. Another positive sign of progress was co-author Tom's unique youth development bachelor and master degrees for prospective and active physical activity professionals offered at the University of North Carolina at Greensboro.

Fraser-Thomas and her associates (Fraser-Thomas, Cote, & Deakin, 2005)—by providing a link between sport and the youth development literature, especially the work of Benson (1997), Lerner (2004), and the National Research Council (2002)—were early contributors to the sport-youth development knowledge base.

As the sport-based youth development movement gained momentum, the broader youth development field began to acknowledge its existence. The first major sign of this shift was the 2007 issue of *New Directions in Youth Development* titled "Sports-based youth development." The seven chapters in this issue covered a range of youth sport-related issues and recommendations, including the following:

Menestrel and Perkins (2007) pointed out some of the advantages and disadvantages of current youth sport practices as well as a set of principles to move typical youth sport programs toward a youth development perspective, including a strength-based approach, utilization of positive assets, and empowerment of youth in problem-solving. As a specific example, they described Play it Smart (see Petitpas, Cornelius, & Van Raalte, 2008). They closed by advocating adults to help kids become "agents of their own development" (p. 22).

Coatsworth and Conroy (2007) took a similar approach, identifying benefits and problems in after-school physical activity programs followed by guidelines to upgrade the youth development component in these activities. Among their suggestions were small enrollment, a stable and trained staff (easier said than done!), choice of activities to give the less gifted sport opportunities, and a detailed description of key program development components. These program components are familiar to many youth development professionals and include assessment of needs, involvement of the community, program development, staff training, and assessment. As examples of programs that connect sport to academics and life skills, Coatsworth and Conroy cited Going for the Goal (Hodge & Danish, 1999), Play It Smart (see this chapter), and TPSR (see this book!).

Daniels (2007) addressed the difficult issue of competition (translated as winning in the American sport culture), arguing for building cooperation and fun into competitive sport. She emphasized moving from an ego-oriented approach based on who is best or who is better to a task-oriented approach based on each young athlete improving on skills related to the sport. She expanded these definitions by comparing the military model (sport as war), the reward model (the best performers get rewards), and the partnership model, which frames sport as a series of personal challenges which require an opponent who, by providing a challenge, is really a partner.

Perkins and Noam (2007) reported the results of a summit that had as its purpose connecting sports, health, and learning in extended day programs. Summit participants agreed that life lessons learned were more important than sport, a significant shift from the usual rhetoric and practice of youth sport ("We can't forget about winning!" as a recent youth sport conference participant shouted). The authors focused on creating "a setting of developmentally intentional learning experiences" p. 77) which emphasized relationships, specific knowledge and skills, and individual needs.

Berlin and associates (2007) described the program design and content, external relationships, evaluation results, and sustainability of four sport-based youth development programs: Harlem RBI, Tenacity, Snowsports Outreach Society, and Hoops and Leaders Basketball Camp (described further on). All four, while based on different physical activities, promote life skills development, have supportive external partners, and have records of sustainability.

Youth Leadership in Sport and Physical Education

In the youth development literature, youth leadership plays a prominent role as part of its advocacy of youth voice and youth empowerment (e.g., Benson, 1997; Hellison & Cutforth, 1997; National Research Council, 2002; McLaughlin, Irby, & Langman, 1994; Lerner, 2004). McLaughlin (2000) viewed youth leadership as an important component of youth development programs, arguing persuasively that youth leadership is a vital component of youth development whatever the content of the program (e.g., art, drama, sport). Benson's (1990) research on capacity building showed that leadership can enhance social competencies and emphasize the development of positive values, especially if opportunities that help others are offered and personal reflection on the importance of service to others is included.

Examples of Sport-based Youth Leadership Programs

Once physical activity programs began to join forces with youth development, a number of promising sport-based youth leadership programs began to spring up. Here are three examples:

Sports 37 is based on the very successful Gallery 37 program in Chicago. After that program's success, several new programs modeled after Gallery 37 but focusing on different content areas were initiated, including Sports 37. Like the others, Sports 37 was a collaboration of the Chicago Park District, After School Matters, and Chicago Public Schools. It was designed so that high school students who were being paid for their attendance would spend 12 weeks with expert coach-mentors learning how to provide a sport-based service as a mentor to younger kids during the summer Park District programs. Five different sports were initially included in the training. The program targeted students from high schools located in some of Chicago's poorest, most violent neighborhoods.

Under Charlie Tribe's able leadership, Sports 37 learned from early mistakes and continued to improve with each passing year. A comprehensive formative program evaluation was conducted in 1995 by Robert Halpern, a well known youth work scholar, and his associates. The report was in general quite positive, highlighting a number of program achievements and pointing out some areas that needed work.

As the Sports 37 program grew and matured, several components were added. One of these components consisted of two evaluation processes designed to hold students and staff accountable for developing the necessary skills. The first evaluation process was composed of six rubrics, each with several categories, for example, I need a lot of work on this, I'm okay at this, or I'm good at this:

- Teamwork.
- Communication.
- Critical thinking.
- Work skills.
- Demonstration.
- Explanation.

The second evaluation process involved a descriptive list of skills for football, volleyball, basketball, soccer, and baseball-softball, each with the same rubrics as the first evaluation process (e.g., I need work on this).

Perhaps the most important component to be added was job training and placement for older teens who had received Sports 37 training. Two tracks were developed: One for lifeguarding, the other for sports. Lifeguarding included CPR, first aid, and aquatic rescue techniques. The sports track included officiating skills and rules as well as leadership training. Both tracks led to job opportunities in the Chicago Park District and with the Chicago Board of Education in life guarding, officiating, and as recreation leaders and junior counselors.

Another program component discussed during the initial development of Sports 37 but not successfully integrated into the training content until later was a youth development component based to some extent on TPSR (which is described in some detail later in this book). The intent of adding this training was to better prepare youth leaders to mentor and teach young kids within a more holistic and developmental framework.

Project Coach (Intrator & Siegel, 2008) utilized the resources of Smith College in Northampton, Massachusetts, and specific youth development concepts to provide a cross-age leadership sports program for underserved kids in Holyoke and Springfield, Massachusetts. Building on the high level of interest in sport in low income communities as well as a thorough interrogation of the typical "sport builds character" (and similar) claims about sport participation, Project Coach creators Intrator and Siegel concluded—as others have as well—that sport alone cannot carry the burden of these claims. Instead, specific strategies for converting sport into a force for good need to be identified and implemented.

Project Coach was built upon a number of such strategies, including an assets-based approach (Benson, 1997), reliance on "connectors" in the community (Gladwell, 2002), conceptualization and delivery of noncognitive skills training (Rothstein, 2004) which "are fundamental for success in any significant endeavor" (Intractor & Siegel, 2008, p. 19), and a specific program plan that capitalizes on these strategies. That plan, based on input from community insiders, teaches high school students in the community how to coach younger kids while integrating noncognitive skills (which the authors call supercognitive skills to represent the multiple dimensions including cognitive development) into their instruction. Leadership, a key noncognitive principle that can be taught so that it transfers to activities outside of sport, is a core component of Project Coach.

Overarching goals of Project Coach included utilizing sport as a vehicle to teach noncognitive skills that can be transferred to life, viewing young people in the community as "resources to be developed" (Intrator & Siegel, 2008, p. 22), building the capacity of the community by training young leaders and teaching noncognitive skills to children in the community, and drawing on resources in higher education to facilitate community development.

A systematic and ongoing evaluation of Project Self included four sets of procedures, each offering a different lens with which to view the program. These procedures include a fidelity check, collecting data from a formal psychometric instrument, videotaping, and more informal reflections from staff and participants.

Hoops and Leaders Basketball Camp, headed by Aaron Dworkin (Berlin et al., 2007), offered a two week summer camp basketball experience which serve New York City's urban youth. Collaborating with the New York City Department of Parks and Recreation and Big Brothers Big sisters of New York City, Hoops and Leaders has implemented programs in four of New York City's boroughs. The program's stated purpose is to provide campers with "caring mentors, leadership skills, and different educational and career paths" (Berlin et al., 2007, p. 102). Volunteer mentors serve for at least one year, receive training, and take part in every camp session. Refereed basketball games alternate with leadership activities each session, and campers eat meals with mentors in order to build positive relationships. Each day of the two week camp a different leadership theme is introduced and linked to basketball practice and games, discussions, and community service projects. Campers are cautioned about viewing professional basketball as a career option. Instead, guest speakers who are referees, general managers, journalists, broadcasters, agents, coaches, and sports marketers discuss sport-related employment opportunities and needed skills. The program is sustained by diversification of funding and volunteers.

Beyond the Ball was developed by Amy and Rob Castaneda to serve Little Village, a large low income Latino community in Chicago. What began as an effort to get youth involved in something positive has developed into a transformative basketball community program that incorporates many youth development principles—conflict resolution, youth voice, service learning, community building, and leadership.

The Castaneda's, who live in the community, have an "open door policy" for kids in the neighborhood; at night, their home is rarely without kids. From meager beginnings, Beyond the Ball has expanded to a Biddy Ball cross-age leadership program, and most recently to B-ball on the Block, a traveling tournament in both the Latino Little Village Community and nearby North Lawndale, a low income African-American community. With this expansion to North Lawndale, the goal of B-ball on the Block has shifted to sorely needed positive racial relations between the two communities.

Insights and Take-aways

The advent of youth development provided as an innovative way for youth work professionals to address the social, emotional, physical, and cognitive domains of kids' lives, whether they are in the more generic roles of program leader or mentor/counselor, or content-specific roles of teacher or coach. However, despite rapid growth in the youth development literature accompanied by a youth development "buzz," youth development principles have not been widely practiced either in school or extended day settings. Ideas such as empowerment, listening to the voices of children and youth, and treating kids as resources fly in the face of traditional practice.

Nowhere is this observation more accurate than in most sport and physical education programs. Despite character development claims since the early 1900's in the United States, their heritage reflects a strong quasi-military top down approach to "training" kids. These practices have been modified through the years, but it is apparent that youth development ideas were not greeted with open arms by most physical activity professionals. That being said, there have always been intuitive teachers, coaches, and mentors in the physical activity field who figured out on their own that some version of youth development principles made a lot of sense. Unfortunately, the vast majority of these innovators remain "unsung." There may be one or two in youth organizations like the Boys and Girls Club in your community, and maybe one or two who are elementary school physical education teachers, or even a coach who defies the entrenched status quo of organized sport.

But this scene is changing. Sport-based youth development in which youth development principles are embedded in the content, whether soccer or jazz dance or some other activity, has arrived. Moreover, leadership programs emphasizing empowerment and transfer of leadership skills to the wider world have emerged. Opportunities to capitalize on and expand these new trends provide newfound hope for the holistic development of all kids through sport and physical education and especially those living in underserved communities.

This book is one such effort.

3

Youth Leadership, Social Justice, and Citizenship

Leadership is not so much about good leaders and good followers. Rather, it is about having each believe they are the Savior for the other.

—Unknown

To further set the stage for youth leadership programming we want to address two important concepts: *social justice* and *citizenship* for children and youth. The reason for doing this is that we see a connection between work in youth leadership development and the advancement of social justice and citizenship issues.

There is a strong tradition in the United States of youth being advocates for different causes outside institutions or systems of power (e.g., antiwar, civil rights, environmental problems). That is, young people have often been crafting, visioning, and leading social movements, in the name of social justice (Mohamed & Wheeler, 2001). To a large extent, the recent election of the United States' first Black president, Barack Obama, was the result of an unprecedented turnout by young voters. However, many of these efforts by youth and others tend to focus on changing the system or institution in the name of social justice. But leadership for social justice can operate in ways that work within the system so that all individuals have equal say and ownership in social policy and attitude. It is here where your leadership program can begin to cultivate awareness of those ideals found in a fair and just society (Libby, Sedonaen, & Bliss, 2006).

We are fully aware that many of you already direct and teach in programs (e.g., Boys and Girls Clubs, schools, Boy and Girl Scouts,

YMCA, YWCA, church programs) which have mission statements reflecting values supportive of social justice and citizenship ideals. By having personal and social responsibility values be the overlay to your leadership program, you will have created a program that can inculcate the values of the institutional mission. However, adoption of such values by your leaders will depend on how they are embraced by you.

For the eventual purpose of interfacing the qualities of youth leadership development to social justice issues, we will describe some of the main social problems facing youth. The vulnerability of young people to certain social problems will certainly weigh in during your attempts to develop them into caring and compassionate leaders. Roger Harrison and Christine Wise (2005) have helped to identify a number of processes associated with social injustice among youth and families. All of these are especially relevant for underserved youth in large and small ways. They are: (a) *exclusion and unfairness*, (b) *stereotyping*, and (c) *stigmatization*.

Exclusion and Unfairness

Many kids are pushed to the margins of society and deprived of having voice, decision-making opportunity, or access to a variety of resources. Their inclusion into the societal mainstream is well beyond reach. For us, inclusion means participation. That is, being able to have ample opportunities for joining and engaging in life activities that nurture personal and spiritual growth of young people.

Unfortunately, exclusion (or inclusion) from a group is too often determined by factors that are not controlled by kids: race, disability, appearance, and economic status. Therefore, avoiding the tendency to unjustly group kids according to these attributes is tantamount to effective leadership development. While social grouping has always been a part of the school landscape—one only has to observe school hallways, cafeterias, playground, and buses to see how grouping is manifested—the level of acceptance by you, the adult leader, will determine how all kids fully engage in your program.

Unfairness is an extension of exclusion. Again, individual differences play an important role in the way kids are taught and assessed. Unfair treatment can be seen in the way they ignore certain kids, fail to address their weaknesses, and fail to adopt realistic levels of expectations. We strongly believe that *all* individuals have the right to be treated fairly—it is a natural assurance of experiencing fairness in making choices and being heard. Lack of inclusion and fairness is not a legislative problem. Rather, it is an adult one where many adults are unwilling to nurture the assets of youth, thus their talents continue to be unrealized. At the heart of these two concepts, then, lies the essence of what effective youth leadership programming can do for kids.

Exclusion and inequality become especially salient when we examine the plight faced by many youth who live in poverty and are nonwhite, especially black children and youth. The interconnection between poverty and youth has been well documented. Studies, especially those done in urban settings, mainly have shown that being poor results in negative and unhealthy behaviors (Hayden, 2007; Harrison & Wise, 2005; Barry, 2005). Richard Lerner and his colleagues (Lerner, Taylor, & von Eye, 2002) believe that the probability of engagement in adolescent problem behavior (e.g., delinquency, violence, unsafe sex) is associated with poverty, and race is the single best predictor of poverty and behavioral outcomes (Lerner, Taylor, & von Eye, 2002). For example, in Guilford County, North Carolina 70% of the suspensions are doled out to Black students—a population that makes up 40% of the students in the county. Furthermore, the achievement gap between whites and blacks is at an all-time high in both Guilford County and Chicago public schools. And, the school drop-out rate reaches as high as 70% in poor urban and rural schools that are predominantly Black and Hispanic. This picture does not get any better as we see that these findings have remained unchanged over the past decade.

These above statistics do not suggest that other groups of youth are not susceptible to the unfortunate consequences of social (and academic) isolation. One only has to be reminded of the terrible Columbine tragedy where two white, middle class kids—Eric Harris and Dillon Kleibold—decided that it was time to have retribution for their isolation from peers and school. Tragedies like the Columbine one will no doubt continue to make the headlines of our newspapers and television news hours. However, there are also the multitudes of tragedies that do not make the spotlight. These are the kids who become the "social burdens" in communities; the ones who simply fall through the cracks of an indifferent social system. They regrettably become a drop out statistic, a mark on a police ink blotter, or what Renny Goldman (1996) calls a "disposable children."

We both believe that there is no panacea for social problems due to poverty (Hellison, 2003). People who live in poverty find that inadequate parent education, poor or no health care, sub-par educational experiences, political and geographic isolation, and lack of opportunity are part of the status quo of the poor.

We have seen hundreds of kids come into our gyms who have responded in numerous ways to institutional failures in their schools and society in general. Unfortunately, these ways have further isolated them from the mainstream causing them to seek other ways of gaining some identity in their lives. Gang membership, drug dealing, and prostitution are some of the ways in which youth have tried to "survive" their disconnection from society.

The idea of reconceptualizing our approach to youth development, and youth leadership in particular, become especially important. By arguing that we must help young people practice good habits and decision making, we proclaim a belief that youth are capable of becoming origins in their lives (deCharms, 1976). That is, they are capable of taking responsibility for the consequences of actions and treatment of others—a fundamental tenet of any social justice movement.

Stereotyping and Expectations

A close companion to our discussion about exclusion and inequality is the impact of *stereotyping*. When discussing social justice and youth leadership we cannot ignore the role that stereotyping individuals plays in the process. Throughout this book we continually stress the importance of establishing positive adult leader-leader relationships. Stereotyping plays a significant role in how these relationships can be affected in positive and negative ways. An underlying factor that helps to define positive relationships between you and your leaders are your expectations of them. The way these expectations are communicated to your leaders will not only affect your relationship with them, but ultimately the success or failure of the leadership program.

Rigid views of what particular people are like or misinformed beliefs about what they can do are not uncommon in our communities. Schools are especially notorious for festering negative expectation effects upon their students. Jonathan Kozol's provocative portrayals (e.g., Kozol, 1967, 1992, 1995, 2005) about inner city schools, students, and teachers paint a dismal picture of poor academic student performance, myopic views of possible futures, and creation of custodial school climates. Scripted teaching and over testing have become the new curriculum in schools. These imposed mandates coupled with few resources for schools, teachers, and students have conveyed a "no confidence" message; an expectation that eventually becomes self-prophetic.

A seminal study by Harvard University professor Robert Rosenthal and California school principal Lenore Jacobson (Rosenthal & Jacobson, 1968) showed how expectations can become self-fulfilling in the classroom. In their study they manipulated the teachers' expectations to see if they would become self-prophetic. By giving teachers "bogus" achievement scores expectations for high and low scoring students were created. Their findings indicated that for the lower grades teachers' expectations were associated with "real" student performance. Since that study over 100 more were conducted in the classroom, most of which confirmed the findings of the original Pygmalion study.

An important outcome of these studies was the support given to the idea that segregated schools would set the stage for biased teaching—especially in schools impacted by low income, Black students. Legislation (i.e., Brown vs. the Topeka School Board) forced school boards to make sure that "separate but equal schools" were available to all students regardless of income status or race. In addition, Title IX legislation (equal opportunity/access for girls and women) was also born out of some of this early expectancy research.

Expectations studies in physical education classes and sport settings have also taken place (i.e., Brown, 1979; Crowe, 1983; Martinek, 1983, 1981, 1989a, 1989b; Martinek & Karper, 1986; Horn, 1984). The findings from these studies showed that the self-fulfilling prophecy exists in gyms and athletic fields as well. These studies, like the classroom ones, provided essential guidelines for teachers and coaches that help them overcome negative biasing effects.

As you guide young leaders your bias must be kept in check. By doing this your ideas will be reflective of the passion you have for developing *every* kid's capacity to lead and serve others. This will also enable you to grab their attention and provide them with a sense of purpose. The bottom line is that leadership needs to be viewed as an activity in which any kid can participate. It is not limited to just a few and does not emerge from some elective or selective process.

Stigmatization

Another example of the destructive consequences of social injustice is the stigma that is frequently laid upon the shoulders of underserved youth and their families. That is, they are automatically seen in negative terms because of who they are or some other circumstances. For example, all those who live in public housing where the crime rate is high may be considered untrustworthy, unreliable, and participants in criminal activity. And, yes, race plays a significant role here. Sociologist Neil Thompson calls this form of social blaming "scapegoating" (Thompson, 2005).

Here, again, we revisit the research findings on successful youth development programs. They consistently underscore the importance of looking at youth, not as problems to society, but as potential assets (McLaughlin & Heath, 1993; Benson, 2006). So often we have seen programs, especially those in underserved areas of the community, "blame the victim" by treating kids as though they are the problem. Such a view ignores economic, social, and political factors that impact heavily on youth and families who live in impoverished neighborhoods. This was and still is an important concept to hold onto for program developers. Once program leaders and policy makers decide that kids are not the problem, they will be in a better position to effectively tap into those qualities that give them capacity to contribute to their community (Hellison et al., 2000; Wenger, 2005). When *midnight basketball* (a nationally funded program) first started, its intent was to get "problem kids" off the street and into the gyms—basketball was to become the "magic bullet." While this program got "the problems" off the street it also moved them into the gym. It was not until program leaders decided to refocus their efforts and use basketball as "a hook" to teach important life skills that would tap into the strengths of the kids. After that, the program began to generate successful outcomes. Certainly basketball (or other sports) will continue to be the "magnet" to bring kids to the program. But for those leadership programs that are supported by a set of strength-based holistic values, the ability to keep kids coming back again and again will be insured.

Stigmatization can also be seen at the individual level. This occurs when the group is experiencing issues due to interpersonal conflicts among the members. What happens here is that an individual can become the *scapegoat* of the group. Often it is an individual who is relatively powerless who bears the brunt of difficulties that may arise in a program. This person becomes the release valve for group tensions. Take, for example, a situation that occurred in the Greensboro Youth Leader Corps program. Miguel was a Hispanic youngster who had just joined the Youth Leader Corps program. His school principal encouraged Tom to allow him to be part of the program. He was new to the community and his past school record was not very stellar. He had a quiet personality and his need to belong made him vulnerable to connecting to the "wrong crowd." At first he seemed to be well liked by the other youth leaders who were all Black. However, when the group went through a period of tension and conflict, the situation changed markedly. Some of the more influential members of the corps began to take out their frustrations on Miguel. Conflict quickly started to occur between Miguel and several of the youth leaders. Many of the youth leaders were blaming Miguel for a variety of problems. This form of stigmatization gave Tom and his staff a major challenge to confront, but one that was necessary given the unfairness of the situation.

The negative and potentially destructive examples of social injustice and oppression expressed in the above examples illustrate the unfortunate consequences of social power. These are all part of the dynamical processes that occur in youth leadership work. Because they are also part of our everyday lives we have a tendency to ignore them. And, yet, they are profound moments for kids who are the oppressed. Therefore, we need to make every effort to attend to them and not leave them unnoticed.

Youth Leadership and Citizenship

An important consideration that must be made in our discussion of youth leadership is citizenship. We feel that an ultimate of outcome of any leadership program, regardless of how remote it may seem, is to infuse a spirit of citizenship in kids. Citizenship represents a viable factor of your leadership program that will help to draw the leader-community gap closer together.

The term citizenship has a multitude of definitions; most often they pertain to actions like obeying laws, voting, and being up on current events. Typically, these attributes are tied to national interests and politics (Sherrod, 2006). But citizenship can be found within smaller contexts like churches, various community programs, schools, and even your own youth leadership program. Concern for others and other forms of altruism also represent critical elements of citizenship. It is this final point where the concept of citizenship interfaces with the responsibility model (TPSR) and our approach to youth leadership development. Simply stated the idea of citizenship not only brings with it the notion of personal responsibility but social responsibility. Sport sociologist Tony Laker (2000) contends that the right to peaceful existence and justice are only tenable when one is able to apply the concept to others. If this is true, and we believe it is, your youth leaders could become the possible change agents needed in a more caring and compassionate society.

For all of this to happen, a healthy interplay between leadership, TPSR values, and character of young people should contain four basic elements. The first is a sense of *moral and social responsibility* (Laker, 2000; Damon, 1990; Shields & Bredemeier, 1995). Throughout this book you will be reminded that in order to get kids to a point in their lives where caring for others is a valued personal quality, leadership experiences based on developmental principles must be applied. The stages of leadership development, which serve as the core of the book, are created with the assumption that each experience serves to scaffold kids to a higher sense of accountability. The development of personal and social responsibility thus becomes the "gateway" to citizenship and access to social justice.

The second element is *community involvement.* For years youth have been considered a segment of the population most likely to refuse to be part of the status quo (Sherrod, 2006). For underserved youngsters, the opportunity to enter the societal mainstream is even more remote. Here the search for identity and possible futures become mechanisms for getting youth to willfully become civically engaged. It would be foolhardy to expect that every young person will rise to a level of civic engagement where they become political activists and policy makers. What we can do, however, is give them a sense of purpose in their own community. This may eventually nudge them into such things as community service, religious and other community memberships, or even changing the conditions of their own neighborhood.

Farfetched? Perhaps. Anthony Triplin, a past leader from the Greensboro program, didn't think so. Anthony decided to run for one of the county commissioners' positions on the city council. He even had a campaign manager! His platform? Getting sidewalks laid down in some of the neighborhoods of his district. He didn't win (didn't even come close), but his initiative for trying to make a difference in his community illustrates a small example of a leader taking it outside the gym. Although Anthony's story is extremely rare for underserved kids, it underscores something that Don heard someone say, "It only takes one case to make a possibility."

The third element of citizenship is *political literacy.* By political literacy we *are not* necessarily talking about having kids know about all of the legislative branches of our government or values and nuances of party affiliation, or the make up of community governance—although knowing about these is helpful. What we are really talking about is having a sense of what it takes to carve personal pathways toward gaining true citizenship status in one's own community. The youth leadership program that you develop will be a great starting point for giving kids "the compass" needed to cross over the borders of indifference, bias, and skepticism. In a way, the values and expectations guiding your leadership program will have created a "political framework" in which the leaders will be more apt to understand. Thus, they will be in a better position to accept or not accept the framework. Knowing how to successfully function within this framework will better equip them with a set of skills and confidence to successfully respond to societal norms in a positive and proactive way.

The final element of citizenship closely aligned with political literacy is *activism*. History informs us that activism played an instrumental role in various social movements (e.g., right to vote, equal and fair educational opportunities, Title IX). And yet, your youth leaders' ability to initiate comparable changes in societal structure will probably be way beyond their grasp. However, what you can do for them is have them adopt a set of values that will enable them to view the inequalities of social injustice in a more informed way. As an adult leader, you can accomplish this by having your leaders lead others in ways that reflect TPSR values. By doing this you will have placed them in a position where they can "plant seeds" of change in others—they become activists of sorts. These seeds will hopefully germinate into those personal attributes defined by respect and fairness to others, overcoming challenge, being self directed, leading and caring for others, and improving community wellness.

As you read on in this book you will discover that no matter what you think young people can do or not do, any success will depend on a certain type of leadership from you. It's the type of leadership needed in not only running a program effectively but it is the kind that will seep into those segments of the community that support and build upon what you try to do with your kids. At the same time, you will continually find that moving kids forward in life will take much more than you can offer. This does not mean that your efforts are going to be wasted. You will need to stay with it—it can sometimes wear you out. Here are a couple of things to be mindful about to help keep you on track.

First, youth leadership programs that include education, learning activities, and service certainly all relate to civic engagement and social justice awareness. However, knowing the type of kids with whom you work will be critical in planning activities. This will be especially true if you are working with kids who come from underserved neighborhoods. For instance, civic engagement for underserved youth who feel marginalized may find community-based experiences much more relevant than any school-based civic education experiences. Many of those "school experiences" often seem too remote from their daily lives because they often involve helping someone outside of their community (Ginwright, Noguera, & Cammarota, 2006). The important point here is that different mechanisms for developing social justice and citizenship in diverse youth must be considered. These mechanisms are activities that should relate to their neighborhoods, family, and community.

A second point is that by embracing a set of values like TPSR, you become prepared to be an activist with a type of orientation needed in a democratic society. By approaching youth leadership from a developmental perspective and by empowering them to lead others, you will have created the perfect venue to engage them in civic life. You will have given them the responsibility of teaching others to be socially and personally responsible through physical activity—a small taste of civic engagement. Underestimating this aspect of your program may cause you to lose sight of the potential that your program has in nurturing a young person's willingness (and need) to change things beyond the gym.

Insights and Take-aways

Getting kids to step up and lead others has implications for creating a moral and just society. This chapter provides a backdrop for viewing youth as possible vanguards for social justice and community engagement. To keep this in mind, here are some things to think about:

- Whether your program resides in institutional settings like schools, clubs, recreation centers, of these institutions are potential homes for leadership programs, leadership development will play a role in supporting ideas for social justice and citizenship. Approaches to foster social justice and citizenship will vary according to the setting.
- Inclusion, equality, stereotyping, and stigmatization are important processes found in social justice issues. These processes are evident in numerous places of a young person's community. They also impact the moral health of the community. More importantly, awareness of these processes needs to be heightened within your youth leadership program.

- Your expectations for kids will be communicated in ways that impact the self-perceptions of your leaders. They can become self prophetic. Awareness of the way you interact with your leaders is an important first step in avoiding negative outcomes from low and sustained expectations.
- Your leadership program can spark young leaders' interest in serving their community. By leading others from their community and instilling a set of values, they will have contributed, in a small way, to the health of their community—a form of citizenship. The successful interplay of TPSR values and character will rely on four elements of citizenship being present: (1) moral and social responsibility, (2) community involvement, (3) political literacy, and (4) activism.

II

Stages of Youth Leadership

4
Stages of Youth Leadership Development

To lead people, walk beside them...As for the best leaders, the people do not notice their existence. The next best, the people honor and praise. The next the people fear; and the next, the people hate. When the best leader's work is done the people say, "We did it ourselves."

—*Lao Tzu*

Developing caring and compassionate leaders (a focus of TPSR goals [levels] four & five) has been a natural progression of our work in the sport and coaching clubs described earlier in chapter 1. Don's book, *Teaching Responsibility through Physical Activity* (Hellison, 2003), has been a mainstay for us and many others who plan and teach values-based physical activity programs. The levels of responsibility described in his book were described in chapter 1. The levels have often been referred to as goals and have given us pathways for running and evaluating our values-based programs. Therefore, it made sense for us to give club participants opportunities to apply the levels (goals) in a more advanced way—by leading others. The TPSR model continues to be the foundation of what we do in preparing kids to become caring and compassionate leaders.

Knowledge of effective teaching strategies is also important. This includes knowing how to plan in thoughtful and simple ways as well as being confident enough to make those "on-the-feet" instructional decisions. Having a sense of what it means to be a responsible human being also helps here. Although a few leaders may have a natural way of working with others, most need careful guidance from you. What has helped us is to first acknowledge that students differ from each other in the way they assume leadership roles and respond to experiences that help prepare them for advancement.

The following overview of developmental stages and themes helps to create a vision or goal toward which the student can strive. First, we present four stages to help you know where kids are in their leadership development. We then describe five themes, that, when consistently applied, insure the students' growth as leaders.

Stages of Leadership Development

To guide you in creating learning experiences for leadership development are a set of developmental stages. Formed by informal observation, an accumulation of various data, and constant self-reflection, these stages have evolved from our work with kids (see Martinek, Schilling, & Hellison, 2006). For us, the leadership stages were an outgrowth of running TPSR-based sport programs. They are built on the foundation laid by TPSR and especially on the fourth level of responsibility, helping and leading others. However, it is not necessary for you to travel the same path. We have met a number of physical activity professionals who have intuitively realized the importance of basing their kids programs on holistic developmental principles that support personal and social/moral development which are very much in the spirit of TPSR but without all the language and nuances. Such programs provide a strong platform for launching the leadership stages.

Table 4.1 Stages of leadership development

Stages	Description
Stage One—Learning to take responsibility	Students learn to respect others, participate and persevere, be a team player, become more self-directed, and begin to explore leadership roles.
Stage Two—Leadership Awareness	Students begin to see themselves as leaders and begin thinking of larger responsibilities of leadership.
Stage Three—Cross-age Leadership	Students are ready to teach physical activities and responsibility values to younger children from community agencies. Planning, teaching, managing behavior problems, and evaluating lessons are now part of their roles.
Stage Four—Self-actualized Leadership	Students are ready for "outside the gym" opportunities to help them reflect more on personal interests and possible futures.

Ultimately, the stages help to build a more holistic view of leadership for the adolescent. In a sense, each stage represents a set of strategies that are stepping stones for acquiring habits for helping and leading others. Table 4.1 shows these stages. Although the stages appear to be sequential, they can also be quite fluid. That is, individuals can experience one stage and then have to revisit the previous stage when faced with new and old challenges. The four stages will also guide you in the planning and evaluation of learning experiences that, in a loose way, build upon one another. Strategies for getting students to experience each stage are provided in the following chapters with ways of modifying them to fit your situation.

Stage One—Learning to Take Responsibility

Because our approach to leadership is based on learning to become personally and socially responsibility (TPSR), stage one focuses on helping kids learn to take responsibility for their own development and well-being as well as contributing to the well-being of others. These are no small tasks for most kids. Socially, they require developing relational skills and values, learning to share their perceptions and ideas for betterment of the group, and helping to make the program a better place to be for all participants. Personally, they need to learn the importance of effort in being successful in any endeavor and to set and work toward personal goals.

These skills and values—learning to respect others, to participate and persevere, to be a team player, to become more self-directed, and to learn how to appropriately support and help others—can be woven into a leadership program or, as we have done, by developing responsibility-based sport clubs. Club members who learn the basics of being responsible can then move on to a leadership program that focuses on stages two, three, and four, at first taking on bite-sized leadership roles followed by cross-age leadership and eventually working as leaders in the community.

Stage Two—Leadership Awareness

In general, adolescents have a distant (and sometime distorted) view of leadership. At the same time, you will find that most will have a natural desire to be helpful to others for a variety of reasons. Making the connection to being responsible for another's welfare (even development) requires a starting point. Helping, teaching, and coaching a fellow club member or classmate takes place at this stage and provide a starting point for more advanced levels of leadership. Getting students to adopt and be successful at these helping roles will require guidance and support from you. How you plan and assign roles, follow-up with feedback, and carve out time for personal reflection all come into play here.

There is another important outcome to this stage of leadership. Besides having the opportunity to lead or teach a peer, kids will benefit another way. They will learn to be good followers. For us, leading and following go hand-in-hand. That is, to be a good leader an individual needs to know how to follow and learn from others. Bob Horrocks, a middle school teacher in Greensboro, North Carolina, always had students rate how well they were lead by their classmate and how well they followed. The intent was to have them cooperate, trust, support, listen, and share in the leadership experience.

Stage Three—Cross-age Leadership

The responsibility of leading broadens significantly during this stage. Planning, teaching, managing behavior problems, and evaluating lessons are now part of the advanced leadership roles given to adolescent leaders.

As described in chapter 1, both the Greensboro and Chicago programs use "veteran club members" to plan and teach physical activities and responsibility values to younger children from community agencies. Others have done this, too. In Denver, for example, Nick Cutforth used cross-age leaders from a junior high school to work with low income minority elementary-age children. Likewise, Dave Walsh runs a cross-age mentoring program in one of San Francisco's elementary schools. In Charlotte, North Carolina, Dan McLaughlin had some of his most responsible fifth graders teach second and third graders during a special lunch time sport program.

It is also during this stage where sensitivity and inner strength to be truly caring and compassionate leaders begins to be internalized. By providing well-intended service to others understanding and valuing the interdependence between the self and others (Gilligan, 1982) are realized. That is, your leaders begin to adopt an ethical concern for their relationships with others; their skills and talents and ability to help others are interconnected. However, it is important to remember that, although leaders can experience the joys of helping others, they also can experience frustration and reluctance that even veteran school teachers experience. This is especially true when they are working with a tough group of children. As one of Tom's youth leaders said during a post-session group meeting: "These kids are really bad, they are ghetto...let's get rid of them!!" The leader's comment reminds us that the challenge to teach all types of kids will be daunting for some leaders. That is why it is important for you to assure your leaders that help is always available to help them through the tough spots. Sometimes that assurance can be both subtle and, yet, poignant. For example, a response to a similar comment by a Chicago youth leader: "They don't listen and they don't do what you tell them" was Don's smile and a one-word comment "well?" That's all it took to make the point.

Stage Four—Self-actualized Leadership

Seeing the success that our leaders were having in working with younger kids, we began to realize that many were ready for more extended experiences. Thus, a fourth stage of development became apparent to us. Various experiences were added to the youth leadership program. They provided "outside the gym" opportunities to get kids to reflect more on personal interests and possible futures (McLaughlin & Heath, 1993).

Oftentimes, community connections become a central player during this stage of development. In Greensboro, for example, "career nights" and summer internships are offered to Tom's Youth Leader Corps members. Various businesses leaders and professionals participate in both events. They not only learned something about a job, they learned how to be with people, how to be on time, and so on. In Chicago, Dave Walsh's Career Club (Walsh, 2008) incorporated peer coaching and apprentice teaching experiences to introduce the concept of careers ("possible futures"). His primary goal was to help leaders find ways to envision greater career choices. And Chicago's Stein Garcia developed a martial arts video with his middle school kids to promote self control and nonviolence in schools. All of these programs will nudge your leaders closer to becoming the new social capital (Putnam, 2000) of their community. Chapter 8 provides various ideas on how to set up and manage these types of experiences.

Themes for Advancement

Advancing students from one stage to the next requires guidance and ideas.

The following sections represent five themes that should be applied within each developmental stage. They are *power sharing, self-reflection, relationships, transfer,* and *integration.* The themes are the necessary "ingredients" of the four stages. In essence, they offer a type of insurance for moving the heart, mind, and soul of a young person closer to being the type of leader we want to see—one who is caring and compassionate.

Power Sharing

We believe that power sharing is neither giving power freely to others nor ignoring our own power (responsibility) to guide others in making the right choices.

Youth workers often fall into the trap of thinking that we empower youth by merely shifting all our decisions to them. This is especially damaging for those who are not ready for such decisions. Power sharing is about giving meaningful and genuine voices and choices in our leadership programs. Our goal has always been to get young leaders to be critically engaged and autonomous. Richard deCharms (1976) sees this as getting them to do as they must rather than as they please even when faced with external forces. In your program you will find that choices can come in different shapes and sizes. Some include choosing the activity and age group to teach, equipment to use, and length of lesson. But for us there are also those choices that come from the heart as well as the mind. Choosing how to treat others, handling conflict and adversity in a thoughtful way, and responding to another's struggles are choices that determine the character of one's leadership.

The Greensboro program has relied on three principles of power sharing (Schilling, Martinek, & Tan, 2001). The first is that power sharing takes on different forms for different people. Not all kids are ready or want to make decisions and, therefore, giving them at the wrong time can backfire. Conversely, there are some kids who are capable and eager to assume large amounts of responsibility or take on roles requiring some level of leadership. And there are times when you have to take away decisions when a leader decides to slack off. This can cause problems which have to be immediately dealt with. If they aren't, the idea that responsibility and leadership goes hand-in-hand will slip away. The bottom line is that you need to have a "good read" on your students and be prepared to give and take away when needed.

Empowering kids also requires you to consider a given situation—the second principle. This principle was often applied when we tried to empower kids in our elementary and middle school clubs. For example, we found that "peer teaching" works best for elementary club members. For the middle school kids, however, we provide a more advanced opportunity for power sharing. They are further along the power sharing continuum. As mentioned earlier, many of the middle school kids are not only ready to teach skills, but also to assume responsibility to run a team practice, organize and oversee a game, and even foster good moral judgment along the way.

The third principle is to be constantly aware that decision making for kids can be an uneven process (McDonald, 1992). Some kids will be incredibly responsible one day (having their teaching area ready to go) and then regress the next (they are nowhere to be found while children are filing into the gym). This is the nature of kids. For those kids that decide to slack off power sharing may need to be reduced. Kids won't like it but they need to know that being a responsible leader means being focused on the job at hand. A great strategy here is to apply Don's "accordion principle" (Hellison, 2003), where responsibility can be given out and taken away according to the readiness level of the leader. A key point here is that power sharing means giving kids genuine choices where guidance in making the right decisions is close at hand. As you read through the next four chapters you will learn how various power sharing strategies foster those choices that enhance the leadership qualities of your students.

Self-reflection

Self-reflection is a way of getting leaders to dig deeper into their leadership experience and develop a higher level of thinking. Unfortunately, self-reflection is not something that our kids always want to do. Even the ones who have been exposed to the process in the sport clubs still resist it in the youth leader programs. But we still find it important and continue to integrate it in the leadership experience.

Reflection time usually occurs at the end of our group meeting. Whereas the group meeting is used to assess the day's program, self-reflection is designed so the leaders can evaluate themselves. One simple way is to simply ask leaders to respond to questions by showing a thumbs up (i.e., I was really planned), thumbs down (i.e., my plan was a disaster), or thumb sideways (i.e., my plan was ok but it could have been better). That is, how did they do as a leader for that day? How did they respond to the needs of the group? How well did they plan? Were their goals met? How did they handle any problems? Were they enthused? An even simpler way is to have the leaders raise their hands to indicate "yes" or "no." In later chapters we will describe in more detail a variety of techniques that have been used. Here are some examples of how self-reflection can be facilitated.

- Writing in a journal or notebook.
- Using checklists with various choices for responding.
- Commenting at the end of a workbook.
- Grading and commenting about oneself on an index card.
- Responding orally to questions.
- Writing short stories about personal experiences (something you might arrange with a leader's classroom teacher).

Although reflection usually takes place at the end of a session, it needs to become a continuous process—not always requiring a bunch of prompts (e.g., questions, journal writing, checklists, etc.). Through critical assessment their boundaries for problem-solving ability and moral lives can be expanded. In her book, *The Power of Mindful Learning*, Ellen Langer, a psychology professor at Harvard, talks about the importance of "cultivating mindfulness" in young learners (Langer, 1997). For us, the process of self-reflection generates the mindfulness we want to see in our leaders. In a sense it reminds them that teaching kids cannot take place in a vacuum. In the end, self-examination will not only enhance the leaders' problem-solving ability but significantly widen the boundaries of their moral lives.

Relationships

In both of our programs learning to be a leader is about the "three big Rs"—relationships, relationships, and relationships. In other words, none of the strategies will work unless you develop a certain kind of connection with your leaders. Much has been written about the power of relationships in youth development work (Lerner, Taylor, & von Eye, 2002; Benson, 2006; Matsudaira & Jefferson, 2006; Noddings, 1992). For some people, relationship building is seen as a pedagogical skill. Others view it as an innate charismatic ability. Still others see it as a combination of both. For us, building relationships is all about *trust and respect*. Outside observers of our programs are always amazed at the level of respect that our leaders show for adults and each other. We know this is primarily the result of the respect that we show them. Dennis Littky, director of New York City's Met School said it best: "If kids are going to be respectful, they must be respected." All this translates into a mutual trust for each other. It's the essence of the culture we try to create within our programs. Because *relationship building* will be so important to your work with kids we have devoted an entire chapter to it (see chapter 9).

Transfer

In all of our youth development work we are constantly mindful of the importance of encouraging kids to apply the values and skills learned from us outside the gym. For example, in our sport clubs we emphasize the importance of kids being personally and social responsible in their schools, neighborhoods, and homes (TPSR's Level Five). In leadership programming the idea of transfer from the gym to other areas of life is no less critical.

There are numerous ways of getting kids to apply leadership qualities to other places in their lives. For example, leadership awareness through peer teaching can be extended by having a classroom teacher have the student help in the classroom (e.g., passing out materials, helping a classmate with some work). Or you can challenge kids to see if they can help another classmate, teacher, parent, or school staff during the coming week. The most advance examples of transfer will be described in chapter 8 where leadership serves the larger good of community through some type of service engagement.

Integration

Integration of the strategies must be done in a way that supports the concept of each stage. The next four chapters describe various strategies that will help you advance young leaders through the four stages of leadership development. The concepts of awareness, effective pedagogy, caring and compassion, and community service will be uplifted by thoughtful and intentional planning and application given by you and your staff.

We want to underscore the importance of having these themes as an integral part of your youth leadership development program. Each of the following chapters focuses on these themes in some way. Integration of the stages and strategies will be a constant theme throughout the remainder of this book. In particular, power sharing and self-reflection runs through chapters that represent each stage of development (chapters 5, 6, 7, and 8).

Insights and Take-aways

The TPSR model can serve as a foundation for what you do in preparing kids to become caring and compassionate leaders. Leadership development programming extends the concept of helping and caring for others.

In addition, we talked about how life events can quickly upend the progress made by a leader. Enthusiasm and diligent planning can be quickly replaced by indifference and a lousy attitude. Although this can be frustrating, it's important to avoid getting caught up in these "ups" and "downs." By acknowledging the stage at which leaders operate and by applying strategies that move them to the next level, a commitment to being a leader to others can be realized. For us (and you) there is nothing more enlightening than seeing leaders empathetic and responsive to the nuances of others. One of our leaders said it best: "In working with these little ones, you learn to be patient...they will eventually get it if you don't give up on them."

Before reading on, following are some of the main points for you to think about:

- The stages are as follows: *Learning to take responsibility, Leadership awareness, Cross-age leadership,* and *Self-actualized leadership.* Although the stages appear to be sequential, they can also be quite fluid.
- Power sharing with kids is vital to their understanding of leadership. If you want them to truly assume leadership roles you must let them lead and not follow.
- Self-reflection is critical if kids are to advance through the stages. It gives them an opportunity to evaluate what they did and what needs to be done. It is not a one time thing to do. Rather, self-reflection must be a continuous process.
- The importance of developing and sustaining positive relationships with your leaders cannot be emphasized enough. Without them nothing will work for you.
- Getting kids to transfer their leadership skills (regardless of the stage they are at) helps further cultivate the spirit of service to others beyond the gym walls. Ultimately, this is what it's all about in becoming a truly caring leader.
- Integrating the right strategies into each stage of development helps to insure growth as a youth leader. If this is not done in a thoughtful way the chances for advancement through the developmental stages will significantly diminished.

5
Stage One: Learning to Take Responsibility

I learned that I have responsibility, and they [adult leaders] helped me find it.

—Coaching Club member

In chapter 1, we discussed the core values and beliefs that influence and provide a basis for our approach to youth leadership through physical activity. In this chapter we provide a primer of TPSR for those readers unfamiliar with TPSR. More importantly for the purposes of this book, we show how the first three responsibility levels provide the foundation for our approach to youth leadership.

Responsibility: Cornerstone to Leadership Development

Our work with underserved youth has been guided from the outset by two questions: The first, "What's worth doing?" could also be put this way: "What kind of contribution do we want to make to kids' lives?" The second question, "Is it working?" follows logically from the first. In youth work, one's values, philosophy, grand ideas, and so on only matter if they lead to a positive impact on kids' lives. The problem too often is that practitioners get caught up in the day-to-day problems that arise from kids' problems at home, at school, and with peers as well as difficulties at the site (e.g., the gym is being used for an assembly) or because of the deep culture of the institution that houses the program (e.g., "this is the way we do things"). As a result, one's values and "best laid" plans never find their way into practice.

Our commitment from the outset was to underserved youth which shifted our attention from the development of motor skills, fitness, and game play toward helping kids develop life skills to help them become productive, decent, contributing human beings. To carry these ideas out, we had to create our own version of the Positive Coaching Alliance's concept of being a "double goal coach": We had to be competent at the physical activity content as well as the life skills content, *and* we had to integrate the two.

This process provided our answer to "What's worth doing" in our professional lives, which is best represented by the theory-in-action described in *Teaching responsibility through physical activity* (Hellison, 2003) and related sources. That in turn led us to develop service-bonded inquiry (Martinek, Hellison, & Walsh, 2004), our answer to "Is it working?" In addition to service-bonded inquiry, other approaches to studying TPSR began to appear as well (e.g., Li, Wright, Rukavina, & Pickering, 2008; Martinek, Schilling, & Johnson, 2001; Schilling, 2001; Wright, White, & Gaebler-Spira, 2004; Watson, Newton, & Kim, 2003). (See chapter 13 for a discussion of research.) Recently, Tim Crabbe (personal communication, 2003) summarized a large scale sport and character development study by acknowledging sport's capacity to provide social value for kids, but only if a social and personal development framework is used.

This body of work, often referred to as TPSR (teaching/taking personal and social responsibility), has been in practice in in-school physical education as well as after-school and diversion programs since the 1970's (Hellison, 1978) and now has a presence in most states, some Canadian provinces, and several other countries including Spain, Portugal, New Zealand, and South Africa.

A Framework

The purpose of TPSR is to help kids take more responsibility for their own well-being and for contributing to the well-being of others in a physical activity environment with transfer to life outside the gym. This definition of responsibility is not widely shared. Often, teachers and parents view responsibility as "doing as you are told," or, in a definition used in a scholarly study, conforming to norms, social rules, and role expectations (Wentzel, 1991).

A loose progression of responsibility levels assigned to the kids (see chapter 1) along with specific responsibilities given to the program director, a specific daily format for the program, suggested

Table 5.1 Levels of responsibility

1. Respecting the rights and feelings of others (self-control)
2. Participation and effort
3. Self-direction
4. Helping others and leadership
5. Outside the gym

Daily format
1. Relational time
2. Awareness talk
3. Planned physical activities
4. Group meeting
5. Reflection time

Program director responsibilities (themes)
1. Develop positive relationships with students
2. Empower students (gradually)
3. Promote self-reflection in students
4. Embed TPSR principles and strategies in the planned physical activities
5. Teach for transfer outside the gym

instructional strategies that embed taking responsibility in the physical activity content, and strategies for specific problems and situations that arise are summarized in table 5.1.

The Role of Sport Clubs and Physical Education Programs

This framework, by providing the basic training for eventual youth leadership, is *Leadership Stage one, Learning to Take Responsibility.* Our approach has been to create TPSR-based sport clubs and physical education programs that focus on the first three responsibility levels and introduce levels four and five. These responsibility levels are described below. As you will see, the first three levels of responsibility provide the building blocks that lead to Level Four, leadership and Level Five, transfer outside the program (or self-actualized leadership).

Student Responsibilities

Participants in the program are asked to take responsibility for working toward the five responsibility goals or developmental levels. These levels progress from very basic to more advanced responsibilities and are useful in program planning and implementation. While all of these goals are central to the TPSR framework, the first three levels provide the foundation for leadership levels four and five (see chapters 6, 7, and 8).

It should be noted that all of these levels are provisional in the sense that their validity depends ultimately on students valuing and trying to put them into practice. To be fully empowered, they must decide to what extent they will accept, modify, or reject them. They are asked to take them seriously, learn them, and practice them before making any judgments about relevance for their lives.

Level one, respecting the rights and feelings of others, is the least someone can do for others. It addresses learning how to control one's self so that the fundamental rights and feelings of others are protected. That includes issues such as physical and verbal abuse (e.g., name-calling and making fun of others), intimidation/bullying, dominating equipment and space, and the inability to control one's temper or resolve conflicts peacefully. Level one requires the creation of a respectful climate in the gym (or playing field) as well as protection of kids' rights, for example the right to fully participate in the activity. Participants also need to learn when it is appropriate to stand up for themselves rather than be controlled by others. While they are not asked to help others at this level, they do need to learn how to "get along" with others, to be a team player whether in a sport or other activity. Student defense mechanisms come into play at this level, for example denial or blaming others. The point is to help students become respectful of others *without direct supervision*—to enable them to practice self-control of their attitude, their temper, and what they say to peers on their own. Adult leaders in this approach work toward helping kids to intrinsically value these ways of being.

Level two, participation and effort, focuses on helping students take responsibility for their own motivation. To take responsibility, students need to be given some, for example, choices of adjusting the task so that it is challenging but not out of reach. For example, they may choose how many pushups and sit-ups they need to do to overload the involved muscles. One choice is how the student will define success. The culture often defines success as winning and in beating others, but many other legitimate definitions could be chosen, such as improvement, task mastery, or achievement of personal goals. Participation and effort include trying things that are unfamiliar as well as learning to persist in an activity that is particularly challenging. Participation also requires cooperating with peers who are also in the program, sometimes on teams, sometimes sharing equipment and space. This builds on and extends level one's right to participate.

Level three, self-direction, is the beginning of advanced student responsibilities. Self-direction recognizes the diversity of their talents, needs, and interests as well as their capacity to choose their own paths not only in physical activities but in life skills as well. Self-direction begins with learning to work without direct supervision, and eventually advances to individual goal setting to meet their own developmental needs, interests, and talents in the four domains (physical, social, emotional, cognitive). Goal-setting includes setting goals that are under their control (e.g., winning is not) and being realistic (e.g., "Instead of making it to the NBA, how about improving your jump shot?"). Similar to level one, to achieve self-direction students need to learn to stand up for their right to pursue their own goals rather than those of their peers.

Level four, helping others and leadership, asks participants to value, develop, and practice the interpersonal skills of sensitivity, responsiveness, caring, and compassion in dealing with others. It asks them to help others without expectations of extrinsic rewards as well as without being arrogant or judgmental. It asks them to listen to their peers, only offer help if it is wanted, and help others to solve conflicts peacefully. Level four can be as simple as saying "nice job" to a peer and meaning it, or by helping everyone have a more positive experience simply by having a positive attitude. The most advanced aspect of level four is to become a leader who possesses all of these qualities.

Level five, transfer outside the program, which includes being a role model for others, is the most difficult to do, but is also the most important. If we have only succeeded in making the physical activity program responsibility-based, we have failed to fully carry out our holistic and developmental values. However, transfer "outside the gym" must be a decision made by the students in relation to their own lives. There are at least two reasons for this. First, the outside world may not support the utilization of these responsibilities. In fact, our kids often report that their classroom teacher, situation at home, and/or peers on the street actively oppose the values and beliefs of the program. It takes more courage than many students can muster to stand up to this pressure without support. The other reason is that ultimately to be truly responsibility-based as we have defined it, students must be the judges of what will work best in their lives and with their aspirations and issues. Remember, these levels of responsibility are provisional, and must be validated by each student to work. Transfer is the most difficult level to put into practice not only for these reasons but also because students cannot practice it in the gym (which is why it is often referred to as "outside the gym"). The adult leader can ask students whether they tried any of the levels in other settings and ask for examples, but in an activity environment such discussions must be brief. (Chapter 8, Self-actualized Leadership, describes a variety of ways to implement responsibility level five.)

These five levels of responsibility also represent skills and dispositions needed to become a youth leader. Levels one and two are essential qualities for a youth leader to possess and demonstrate or model for those he/she leads. A leader without self-control, self-motivation, and/or a cooperative attitude can only lead others in the wrong direction. A leader also needs Level three, self-direction and more specifically the ability to set and carry out goals. Level four includes leadership, thereby providing an advanced status for students in a TPSR program. Leadership stage one, *Learning to Take Responsibility*, focuses on this developmental progression and especially levels one, two, and three.

Format

All other components of the framework—the daily format, adult leader responsibilities, strategies to embed responsibility in the physical activity content, and strategies to address problems and situations—support *Stage one, Learning to take responsibility*, and are often useful in the more advances stages of leadership as well.

The daily format ensures that taking responsibility is addressed every day and that kids receive an opportunity to reflect on their attitudes and actions as well as have a voice in program planning and evaluation. The format consists of five parts, one of which—the planned physical activities—occupies most of the program's time:

- Relational time to enable the adult leader—that's us and perhaps you—to briefly interact individually with program participants at the beginning of the program.
- An awareness talk to emphasize the students' responsibilities (the five levels).
- The planned physical activities with TPSR principles and strategies embedded in the physical activity content.
- A group meeting to provide participants with the opportunity to critique/evaluate the program that day and to offer solutions to issues that they raise. You talk last—if at all. This time is devoted to the kids' reflections on the day's experiences and for them to share their observations about the program that day. Program directors are there to listen, monitor the process (e.g., so everyone is respectful), and comment at the end if needed.
- Reflection time so that participants can evaluate themselves in relation to their responsibilities (the levels)—e.g., were they respectful of others or do they need some work on that? If they need work, that can become a goal in the goal-setting process at level three.

To explain these parts of the format in more detail, relational time gives the program leader an opportunity to interact individually with as many students as possible before the organized part of the program begins. The primary goals are to convey to individual kids that they have strengths as well as things that need work, that each is a unique individual, that each has a voice that the program leader is willing to listen and respond to, and that each student has the capacity to make decisions. These conversations are brief, sometimes as the program leader walks by a student—for example just noticing some new shoes, commenting on a contribution the student made in the last meeting, asking if he/she is willing to be a youth leader today or, on the other hand, "can you pick up the pace a little compared to the last meeting?" You can plan for these little talks by deciding before the program begins what student assets, issues, or individual characteristics might be worth a small conversation.

The awareness talk's purpose is to gradually introduce students to the levels and request that they take responsibility for not only knowing them but putting them into practice. Once they know the levels, you can ask for volunteers to tell the group what this program is really about in their own words. By teaching or reminding peers about their responsibilities, participants are beginning to assume the role of youth leader. Helpful tips for most adult leaders—and sometimes the kids—are the "ten word rule" and the question-answer ratio. The ten word rule states that you have ten words to make your point. There are three reasons for this rule: First, adults who assume leadership positions in kids' programs often talk too much, long after students have "checked out." Second, the awareness talk meeting should be brief. And third, being brief and to the point gives potential youth leaders a model when they assume leadership roles. Of course, it isn't really a ten word *rule*, because more words are often necessary to make a point. But it does emphasize the need to keep it short. Another tip is the question-answer ratio. Both adults and kids tend to tell rather than ask. Questions tend to engage students; statements tend to be ignored. The point is to achieve a balance between the two.

The planned physical activities, just like the other parts of the daily format, need to be responsibility-based. A few examples make this clear:

- Direct instruction is useful at level one to teach protection of the rights and feelings of everyone, for example, by requiring a certain number of players on offense to touch the ball before it can be shot in team sports such as basketball, soccer, and lacrosse (or sent over the net in volleyball),

the number depending on players' skills and the number of players on a side. The point is to ensure that *all* kids get involved. Over time, the rule can be relaxed, because students learn that cooperating with all teammates is part of the game.
- At level two, you can modify tasks (drills) in two ways to shift responsibility to students (and promote self-motivation): First, by allowing them to modify the task so that it is more or less challenging depending on their skill level, and second, by making the tasks self-paced so that they can move from one station to another on their own as they complete the tasks.
- Also at level two, participants can be provided a choice in game play, for example, a highly competitive game in which winning is prioritized, a game that places emphasis on cooperation and playing as well as they can rather than on the score, and a practice area for students who decide they are not ready to, or not interested in, playing a game.
- Level three activities include the option for kids to work on their own on a prescribed task without direct supervision, as long as they are responsible enough to work independently. An advanced form of level three is to introduce a goal-setting progression so students can choose their own goals, make a plan, attempt to carry it out, and evaluate its success.
- Level four focuses on helping others and leadership. The first step in this process could be reciprocal coaching (adapted from Mosston & Ashworth, 1994) in which students pair up for a drill with one student as the coach and the other the player. The coaches, armed with a few simple cues for the task (e.g., shooting the basketball or soccer ball, passing a volleyball), assist their player partners by observing the assigned task (e.g., basketball shooting or throwing a ball) several times while giving feedback about the players' performance in relation to the cues. Then the coaches and players switch roles. (See chapter 6, *Leadership Awareness*, for more information regarding reciprocal coaching and other strategies.)

The group meeting at its best offers an often-rare opportunity for students to gain "experience in deliberating about the common good" (Power, 2002, p. 134). Just asking students what they liked, if anything, and/or disliked, if anything about today's program is one way to get started. If time is short, they can remain standing while a couple of them volunteer one of their likes or dislikes. Then others can be asked to raise their hands if they agree with what the volunteers said. This way, they are given a voice without taking much time, and the program director gets a sense of their preferences. Eventually, when youth have leadership roles, they can be asked first "how it went today" with their team or group, then the other students can share their views. Often, issues are raised. One rule is not to blame anyone by name; instead, share the problem without names. When issues are raised, others should be asked for suggestions to fix the problem, again without names. Participants can be asked who made positive contributions to others today, including saying "nice job" to someone, paying attention to the youth leader's instruction, solving a conflict, or helping someone with a skill or problem. They can also be asked how we, the adult leaders, could do a better job. Since students are rarely (very rarely) asked to evaluate an adult, this question will take some explaining and coaxing. But it will also make the adult leader more human. For the group meeting to work, you must be careful not to share your observations about the day until students have talked. Then you can speak to share observations and/or comment on the group's discussion if necessary.

While the group meeting involves evaluating the program, reflection time emphasizes the kids evaluating themselves, and more specifically how well they carried out their responsibilities (the levels). The questions can be simply stated, for example, "how was your self-control today? Your teamwork? Your effort? Did you set any goals for yourself? Did you help anyone today? How was your self-control in school since we last met (outside the gym)?" Their answers can be verbal, written, or indicated by a physical gesture such as raising hands or using thumbs pointed up for "my self-control (for example) was good today," sideways for "my teamwork was okay today," and down for "my leadership needs work." Once again, you talk last, if at all. If someone's self-evaluation seems a stretch, the director may ask for evidence or have a private conversation after the meeting. Both the group meeting and reflection time require that students you in order to give honest responses, something that takes time to develop.

Strategies for Problems that Arise

Several general strategies exist for dealing with problems that arise in the program. Some of these strategies are also useful for youth leaders, for example, using reflection in planning and debriefing a lesson, learning how to reflect-in-action, and making a solutions bank.

Self-reflection involves planning for possible problems before the program and reflecting after the program on what happened and what actions should have been taken for problems that cropped up. One way to prepare is to make a solutions bank (Orlick, 1980) that consists of "If...then" statements in which the "ifs" are problems that could arise, and the "thens" are what might be done to deal with each problem. A solutions bank may not provide suitable answers to problems that do occur, but it prepares you for unexpected possibilities. In the process, it fattens your "bag of tricks." Reflection-in-action (Schon, 1987) consists of making a quick judgment "on one's feet" (i.e., while working with kids) in relation to a specific unanticipated problem. It differs from what Schon calls knowing-in-action, because knowing does not require a creative in-the-moment response. A similar strategy contrasts technical challenges which involve known responses with adaptive challenges which have no clear solution (Heifeitz & Linsky, 2002).

Examples of more specific strategies include:

- The accordion principle, which tightens and loosens empowerment opportunities with each student's ability to demonstrate responsibility.
- Conflict resolution strategies such as sport court elected by students who deliberate and make judgments in the case.
- These abbreviated examples are just a few of many strategies available to deal with problems that arise. Others include a sit-out progression, the talking bench, an adult-directed group, self-officiating, and making new rules (Hellison, 2003).
- Some of these strategies require one-on-one "counseling time" between you and an individual student. Counseling time, in comparison to relational time, focuses on identifying the student's problem, exploring and negotiating solutions, making a specific plan, and follow-up. Examples that often benefit from counseling time include repeated conflicts with others, selfishness ("it's all about me"), low motivation, inability to work independently, and irresponsible leadership.

Adult Leader Responsibilities

If you are now or aspire to be an adult leader of the kind of program we are describing, you will be responsible for putting into practice the levels of responsibility; format, including the integration of specific responsibility-based strategies; and strategies for specific problems and issues that arise. Without their integration into every program session, taking personal and social responsibility will become rhetoric (e.g., "this is a description of what we do in our programs") versus reality (e.g., "what you are observing is kids taking responsibility in our program").

In a TPSR-based program, you have five responsibilities. First and foremost is the need to develop positive relationships with each student insofar as possible. Professionals associated with youth development sometimes refer to this as the three Rs: Relationships, relationships, relationships. Second, you need to gradually shift power to, or share power with, the students. In other words, students need to have ownership in the program. They need to be able to make decisions and to learn from both successes and failures of their decisions. Recent conversations with different groups of adult youth workers suggested that most view empowerment as important but few know how to empower kids.

Self-reflection is the third adult leader responsibility. In *Teaching Responsibility through Physical Activity* (Hellison, 2003), self-reflection was presented as a component of empowerment, because self-reflection is part of the empowerment process of helping students learn to make wise personal and social-moral decisions and giving them opportunities to do so. Tom added self-reflection as a separate theme in his leadership stages, which more fully supports the purpose of TPSR. In subsequent publications and presentations (e.g., Hellison, Martinek, & Walsh, 2007) self-reflection was separated from empowerment and presented as a third director responsibility.

The fourth responsibility is embedding TPSR principles and strategies into the physical activity content. This is exceedingly difficult, because the vast majority of physical education teachers and coaches find that these principles and strategies are very different than most of what they have been doing on a daily basis since they were students and athletes. Those who attempt to implement TPSR report that the awareness talk, group meeting, and reflection time are easier to learn and do than embedding responsibility principles and strategies into the physical activity content. As in all of these ideas, it usually works better to start small, with something you think you and your students can do and then build from there. (See Hellison, 2003, pp. 123–134 for more ideas.)

The final adult leader responsibility is teaching for transfer, implementing one small idea from TPSR. Teaching for transfer is difficult for a couple of reasons. It is practiced outside of the physical activity program, making it difficult to observe in practice, reflect on, and make adjustments, unless someone outside of the program is enlisted to help, such as a classroom teacher, a counselor or social worker, a playground supervisor, and/or a parent. However, transfer can be addressed in the awareness talk as one of the program's goals even though it goes on outside the gym, as well as in reflection time when a couple of minutes can be devoted to reflecting on whether anything inside the program is influencing outside values, attitudes, and/or behaviors. These are beginning steps in the transfer process, which culminates in *stage four, the Self-actualized Leader* (see chapter 8).

Framework versus Spirit

To remind ourselves as well as others interested in adopting the framework, we include the caveat that TPSR is more than a framework with specific things to do; it also possesses a spirit. Nick Forsberg of Regina University in Canada described it not as a way of teaching or running a program but as "a way of being" (personal communication). It is also a way to relate to kids as well as a way to focus on the whole person.

Leadership Stage One: Learning to Take Responsibility

As the first leadership stage, TPSR helps program participants learn to take responsibility and provides a jumping off point for writing this book. Specific examples of first stage youth leadership experiences, as described above, include:

- Learning to put into practice respect for others, self-motivation and teamwork, and self-direction including goal-setting as prerequisites to being a youth leader.
- Contributing to the awareness talk.
- Exploring reciprocal and peer coaching.

TPSR has been used in in-school PE, after-school youth development programs, youth sport, and even in non-sport programs such as elementary school and secondary school classes (e.g., social studies, math). In our work, all our cross-age leaders have previously participated in an extended day sport club as participants (i.e., club members) learning to take responsibility. The "club" concept is emphasized at all times to the students so they feel that they have "ownership" in the program. Don has two clubs called the "Coaching Club" and "Martial Arts Leadership Club" and has had interns run a soccer club, a jazz dance club, and a fitness-nutrition club. Tom's program is called the "Project Effort Sport Club" and encompasses a variety of sports and physical activities. All clubs involve students in physical activity experiences that emphasize taking personal and social/moral responsibility. The club experiences also wean kids into more responsible leadership roles, something that is initiated in Stage one and more fully developed at stages two, three, and four.

In short, developing caring, compassionate, sensitive, and responsive leaders has been central to our work for a long time. The leadership stages are a natural progression of our work with kids.

Insights and Take-aways

- What is the definition of responsibility or "being responsible?" Adult leaders sometimes—perhaps often—define responsibility as "doing what I tell you." TPSR is based on a different definition of responsibility, one which empowers students to take responsibility so that they have opportunities to practice and reflect on decisions made as well as to explore the values involved in the decision-making process.
- TPSR is the foundation for the youth leadership program we envision. Leadership experiences begin here, as students move through the levels of responsibility—reinforced by relational time, the awareness talk, specific responsibilities in the activity program, and group- and self-reflection. This process encourages kids to recognize and act on the need to take responsibility and be accountable for their decisions and actions.

6

Stage Two: Leadership Awareness

You never know when you make a memory.

—Ricky Lee Jones

In chapter 5, TPSR's level four (helping and leading others) represented the beginning of the leadership experience. In both our programs we have always made sure that kids have a reasonable grasp of the first three levels of responsibility (i.e., self control and respect for others, self-motivation, and self-direction). Stage two, *Leadership Awareness*, brings to students experiences that further help them process the interpersonal skills needed to help others. Working at this stage of leadership development initiates a fundamental shift in the way students view their relationship with others. They begin to realize that the focus is now on others—rather than themselves. They begin to recognize and respond to the feelings and needs of others. Child psychologist William Damon underscores the importance of providing the right opportunities that foster such empathic tendencies in children and youth (Damon, 1990). Along with this, both confidence and courage will become the allies for students. These two attributes help to rebut the all too common perception of peers that it is not "cool" to step up and help another.

Because students will have their first in-depth experience in helping and leading others during this stage, it is wise to wean them into to making these social contributions. This is done by presenting a range of simple to more complex helping roles.

Pin-pointing and Acknowledging Leadership

A good starting point for introducing the concept of helping roles is to simply look for examples of leadership. Mike Reeder, a teacher in one of Minnesota's alternative high schools, uses the strategy of "pin-pointing." That is, he looks for acts of leadership that occur during his class sessions. For example, when one of his students helps another or offers to help with equipment distribution, he acknowledges the student's action privately, or sometimes in front of the class. He believes (as we do) that public and private recognition by the teacher or adult leader often adds credence to the leadership action for most kids.

At the same time, it is important to be sensitive to each individual's response to public acknowledgement—sometimes it can backfire on you! Some kids don't want to be singled out. It may be too embarrassing for them. One way to avoid putting the child in an uncomfortable position is to ask him or her if it's okay to talk about the action with the rest of the class. Doing this shows that you understand the student's side of things. Dignity and self worth is preserved and the value of public acknowledgment is insured.

Pin-pointing helping actions doesn't always have to be done by you. During our group meetings or reflection times, we have asked club members to identify those who contributed in a positive way to the club session. You will be amazed at what kids will recognize as helping roles. Identifying a fellow club member who resolves a conflict between two other members or spontaneously shows a club member how to shoot a jump shot or tells a teammate not to "hog the ball" are just a few examples of what kids will bring up given the opportunity. In many ways, peer recognition can have more impact than recognition from the adult leader.

Peer and Team Coaching

Other ways of fostering leadership awareness is through peer teaching and team coaching. Unlike pin-pointing, these two approaches offer more structured opportunities for experiencing leading and helping roles. It is at this stage where you will find that specific pedagogical strategies come into play.

Peer Coaching

In chapter 5 we introduced the idea of using "peer coaching" as a way of teaching the concept of TPSR level four—Helping and

Leading Others. In peer coaching (a form of Muska Mosston and Sarah Ashworth's 1994 reciprocal teaching), students are paired with another student. One is assigned as a teacher who teaches the other a sport skill. Kids can also choose a partner but the choice must be with the intent of helping someone in a positive way. After awhile the roles are reversed. The students learn how to observe and give feedback to a fellow club member who is performing a particular sport skill. However, simply telling them to teach each other without guidance can result in a disastrous and counterproductive experience. Remember, not all kids are a Michael Jordan or a Cheryl Swoopes (although they will tell you they are!). Therefore, providing a few, simple, cues during this "weaning process" will help them immensely in their new role as a teacher. The point here is that guidance will be needed to build the confidence to step up and take on more challenging leadership roles such as teaching two or three peers at a time.

The use of acronyms can help leaders use cues. For example, we have used the term "BEEF" to represent key parts of the jump shot (e.g., balance position, elbows in, elevation, follow through). The kids never forget this word! Also, it becomes a great device to help the learner remember what to focus on. When asked what they did you learn from you coach, they often say, "I learned BEEF!!" The peer coaches can also create their own acronyms. One peer coach came up with the word "FAT" for teaching a basketball lay up (*foot*—use proper take-off foot, *altitude*—jump high and straight, *touch*—use soft touch against the glass).

Another strategy is to have "task cards or sheets" that describe certain cues. Having something written is a good way to start for those who are peer coaching for the first time. These serve as prompts for the coach during the coaching experience. After awhile, giving the cues orally can be just as effective. Table 6.1 illustrates what a task card would include for teaching specific volleyball skills.

Since peer teaching involves a shift of teaching responsibility toward the student, it is important to avoid subverting this new role by not intervening. Every time you step in to teach, the unspoken message is that the teacher is doing an unsatisfactory job. This significantly lowers the legitimacy of the teaching role. We have found that stepping in to assist the peer teacher is a very natural reaction by most adult leaders. The "let-me-help-you" tendency becomes almost habitual. In order to insure that peer teaching becomes an authentic power-sharing experience, adult leaders must overcome this instinct and replace it with subtler means of guidance. Questions like "How is your partner

Table 6.1 Teaching cues for volleyball

Forearm Pass
- Hands/thumbs together
- Elbows Straight
- Knees bent
- Feet should width apart
- Contact point just above hands
- Eyes on ball

Set
- Feet are shoulder width apart and knees bent
- Index fingers and thumbs form window (triangle) with rest of the fingers Spread
- Elbows out and eyes on ball
- Contact of ball with finger tips (soft touch)

Serve (Underhand)
- Body facing target area
- One foot ahead of the other and knees bent
- Arm extended out while holding ball in palm of hand
- Striking hand in paddle shape (top of fingers bent)
- Contact point is at heal of hand
- Follow through after contact

doing?" "How is the position of her feet?" "What do you think he needs to work on?" help guide the peer coach toward areas that may need further work. Judy Twine, a middle school teacher in North Carolina, has a more indirect way to help the teacher. She uses nonverbal gestures to assist her peer coach while standing in back of the performer. For example, she would point to her knee to tell the teacher that he needed to have the performer's knees bent or cup her hands around her mouth to have the teacher speak louder.

There also will be moments when direct guidance is necessary. For instance, if a peer coach is being too critical a negative situation for the learner can be created. Some peer coaches may get "carried away" with correcting the learner. After all, there is a limit to the amount of negative feedback that even the most secure student can withstand.

Reflection also becomes a critical part of the peer coaching process. One way to provide introspection by the students is to have the students share how well the other coached them. You can do this by having them come together in pairs after a coaching session. Or you may have a quick group reflection period after the coaches have finished teaching. We have a couple of ground rules with either form of reflection. One rule is to have the coaches respond first to questions like:

"How did your partner do?" "What were some things that worked for you?" Having the coaches go first helps to affirm the value of their role as a coach and teacher. Then follow up by having the performer evaluate the coaches. You should have some questions ready that specifically focus on the coaches... not the players. Questions like, "How well did you get coached?" "What were some helpful things that the coach taught you (a good way to find out whether the cues were emphasized by the coaches)?" "What were some of the positive things the coach said to you?" "In what way do you think you got better?" Having both the coach and the player respond this way insures that both feel they were helpful to one another.

As kids get more confident with their coaching role, they will be ready to coach a group of peers. This will be especially appropriate for the older elementary and middle school students who are ready to coach a larger group of peers. One way to help them assume this new role is to let them lead the entire class in an activity. One example of this is having a student lead fitness or skill drills at the beginning of class.

Having you demonstrate and provide directions first for them is helpful here. For example, we have used a dribbling drill where the kids follow the dribbling path of the adult leader while in a defensive stance. The "follow the leader" concept continues by asking who would like to lead the group next. Don't worry. Hands will go up and kids love to not only lead but show off.

Later, they can begin to make decisions on what to teach the class. You can also bring in the students who want to lead while the rest of the group is engaged in free play or practice. Giving a few simple directions as to what to do or some written tasks/cues on a note card will help get things started. Initially meetings like these may take a couple of minutes but after awhile the meeting time will become shorter.

Another time that you can have students coach (teach) peers is during station work. Having kids lead in small numbered stations (e.g., 6 to 8 kids at a station) has worked well in our programs. In basketball, for example, you can have a number of stations that focus on specific basketball skills with a peer coach leading at each station. Each coach can then be responsible for teaching that skill to smaller groups of peers. By rotating of the small groups, the peer coach can repeat the lesson. This allows the coach to make changes if needed.

Team Coaching

Team coaching is much like the sport education model developed by Daryl Siedentop (Siedentop, 1994). However, our approach to team coaching differs from sport education in several ways. First, there is less emphasis on the competitive nature of the sport that is being coached. Individual game statistics are not kept, game scores are not recorded, and team standings do not exist in our programs. Rather, fair play, including and respecting the skill and size differences of others, and controlling actions and negative impulses are some of the main issues that our coaches focus in on. In fact, who wins and who loses are rare points of discussion during our group talks. Rather, acknowledgement of who contributed to the team and in what ways the coach helped the team improve are the usual focal points of discussion. A second difference is that coaches are empowered to make decisions about their team and the conduct of the game. There are no referees since we want the players and the coach to be responsible for calling fouls and finding consensus on other game play decisions (e.g., out of bounds and traveling calls).

In team coaching students are asked to run a small practice, monitor a game, and oversee the conduct of fair play. Having some sport knowledge and skill are helpful but not required when selecting leaders. What will be required are these developmental signs:

- A sincere interest in being helpful to a peer. That is, there are caring and compassionate feelings toward the well-being of others;
- Your ability to size up students who can readily take on the responsibility of helping others;
- Inner strength in the student leaders so they can have the courage to make decisions that are not always popular with their peers. For example, leaders need to be able confront those who are fooling around and are not focused (Hellison, 2003, p. 73).

The impulse for some students who are not skilled is to quickly volunteer to coach. However, finding themselves coaching their peers is not as easy as it seems. Frustration and embarrassment can quickly take over their desire to be "in charge." This results in a negative circumstance for both the coach and players. When this happens, the "right to exit" the situation is always there for the student. We ask the leader if she or he wants some help from one of the players. In most cases, the coach is more the willing to relinquish the reigns.

Another thing for you to consider will be the process of determining the composition of teams. Selection of teams can be done a couple of ways...you may add yours to these. One way is for you to make up the teams ahead of time. A more empowering approach is to meet with the

Table 6.2 Team practice plan

First Part (five minutes)—practice drill:
Two-line lay-up drill (one line rebounding the other shooting
Switch lines at half way point

Second Part (five minutes)—go over zone defense:
Two-one-two (stress zone of responsibility) on defense
Offensive positions against zone defense (stress passing and moving)

Third Part (1 minute)—Go over rules:
No pressing
Soft defense
All touch before shooting
Build up—Don't tear down

---

coaches and have then select team members emphasizing that equal distribution of skill is a must.

At the beginning, help from you will be needed in planning the practice. For example, a simple practice plan made out by you is a good way to start. The plan is given during a brief meeting with the coaches while their teams are shooting around. The plan can include a few simple drills, basic rules to enforce, and defensive and offensive patterns. The plan can be given orally or it can be written on card. A scripted plan on a card like the one shown in table 6.2 (thanks to Dave Walsh) is a nice supplement to oral directions. Later, the coaches can create their own practice plans (which will probably look like yours!). Your guidance might also include reminders about calling and conducting time outs and ways of dealing with arguments and misconduct issues.

Another important role of the coach is to monitor the play of the game. We ask coaches to enforce certain rules which (we believe) help the game go well for all the participants. Remember, there will be considerable variability in the skill level of players of a given team. Here are four simple rules that we have used for our basketball coaching clubs in Greensboro and Chicago:

1. *All touch*: All players must touch the ball before a shot can be taken. In soccer we have used a "two touch rule" where players *must* tap the ball two times before passing or shooting. In volleyball, we require a minimum one pass before hitting the ball over the net, while encouraging two passes rather than one. *Rationale*: This insures that everyone is included in the play of the game (respecting the rights of others).
2. *No full court pressing*: Players must go down to the other end of the court after the other team gains control of the ball. Rationale: Kids (especially the less skilled ones) have a difficult time handing full court pressure.

3. *Soft defense*: Back off when guarding a player who is not very skillful. *Rationale*: This gives the less skilled player a better opportunity to make a pass, dribble, and/or shoot during play.
4. *Zone defense*: Both teams must be set up in a "tight" zone defense of their choice (i.e., 2-1-2, 1-2-2, 1-3-1) when defending the other team. *Rationale*: Again, skill level comes into play here. Less skilled (sometimes skilled) kids have a difficult time playing with a player constantly defending them. We have also found the man-to-man coverage results in a lot of "rough play" and trash talk as they try to "out-man" each other.
5. *Positive support and no verbal abuse*—Supporting one another is a must during the games. This often a challenge for the more skilled and competitive players. *Rationale:* "Put downs" don't help kids get better, especially the less skilled. In Greensboro's programs kids are reminded that their responsibility is to "Build up and don't tear down" (a saying contributed by Dennis Johnson—thanks Dennis).

For half court play the rules can be slightly modified in this way:

1. All touch
2. Soft defense
3. No make it take it
4. Take ball back on change of possession
5. Build up—don't tear down

Coaches can help to enforce these rules or other issues by calling time outs to solve defensive and offensive problems and conflict issues. One system that we have used is a two-tiered one borrowed from one of Don's former students, Nikos Georgiadis. Like the NBA, he has the coaches call a 20-second time out for small problems by touching their shoulders. For big problems, they form a T with their hands (See Hellison, 2003).

Players can also call a time out at any time during the game as long as they don't abuse the privilege. At first, you can call the time outs so the players and coaches get an idea of their function and what rules need to be enforced. But this is just a starting point, if needed. The coaches (and players) need to recognize when something is not going well and be responsible for calling the time out. We tell our coaches that if we have to step in, then you are not doing your job! We have seen many kids (young and old) be able to assume this level of responsibility. Getting kids to step up and get control of their team and the game in a positive way are stressed at all times. Some coaches have been able to head things off before trouble starts between two players as well as make sure everyone is included.

Like peer teaching, team discussion and reflection are important end points of the coaching session. Whole group or individual team meetings or both can take place here. In all instances, the peer coaches and then their players are asked to evaluate the practice, the game, and who on their team made positive contributions. Lastly, you, the adult leader, can share your thoughts about their practice and the game. Any comments—especially positive ones—about the peer coaches can be made during this time. The meeting ends with self-reflection by having each team member show thumbs up, sideways, or down as an indication of how he or she did regarding self control, self-motivation, self-direction, and helping others. You should also ask if what they did today can be used outside the gym. Sometimes, the peer coaches and players can evaluate in a less public way. One simple way that we have done this in Greensboro, is to hand each student an index card. On one side they write down a letter grade (A, B, C, D, F) as to how the team did overall and describe (very briefly) the reason for the grade. On the other side, they grade their performance—that is how they contributed to the team along with reason for the grade. They can put their name on the card if they wish or they can leave it off. In some cases, the response may be more honest ones when doing it in a more private way.

Peer leadership in physical activities that do not have teams and games is carried out differently. In martial arts for example, peer leaders volunteer to teach a particular skill such as a side kick or a block to everyone in the program. They are given a cue card for the skill they have chosen and are required to study the cues before attempting to teach (homework!). When they say they are ready to teach, they take over the class for a brief time and later reflect on how well they did with help from the adult leader. Another peer leadership role in martial arts is to be in charge of a station—for example, a kicking station at which the peer leader holds up a large kicking pad and gives the few kids at his or her station instructions to guide them when it is their turn to kick at the target. Then the peer leader gives feedback to each student regarding kicking form.

Insights and Take-aways

Any time you create conditions that force youth to sacrifice their own personal values for the sake of helping another out, inner conflict emerges. Individual values, beliefs, and human purpose come into play where no matter how structured or unstructured you make the experience, the frailty of all three can be easily uncovered. Dealing with the ups and downs as kids try to help others will require you to tightly hold on to your own core values as you create each experience for your kids. Power sharing, reflection, and responsible guidance are now expected by the peer teacher and coach...these expectations, although introduced in stage one, will not be ingrained in most youths' skill sets. So your persistence in guiding your students through this stage of leadership awareness is critical, and thoughtful integration of the strategies from this chapter will be of equal importance. After all, getting students to see themselves as leaders and begin thinking of larger responsibilities of leadership will be your ultimate goal. In order to reach this goal here are some final thoughts from this chapter that you should take with you:

- Stage two—Leadership Awareness—is the jumping off point for applying TPSR values to leadership experiences. It is an extension of TPSR's level four. Students must have a good grasp the concepts underlying the first three levels of TPSR (see chapter 3) to advance to this stage.
- Progression is important to wean the student from one-on-one to group leadership responsibility.
- Reflection and group affirmation are integral parts of the experiences in this stage. Since this will be the students' first in-depth experience being a responsible leader, guidance by you is tantamount to insure deeper meaning of the experience.
- Both younger and older kids are capable of providing leadership to their peers and making good decisions during the process. However, you will need to adjust the experiences so they are developmentally appropriate.

7
Stage Three: Cross-age Leadership

I feel like I am respected because the children listen to what I am saying and they take it to heart.

—*Youth Leader Corps member*

Earlier we described our leadership programs in Chicago and Greensboro (i.e., Urban Youth Leader Project and Youth Leader Corps). We also mentioned similar programs that operate in Denver (Nick Cutforth's Energizer Club) and San Francisco (Dave Walsh's Career Club). All of these programs, while unique in structure have common features to them. First, they all extend the notion of responsibility through leadership experiences. Second, most of the leaders were previous members in their respective sport clubs. And third, they were able to see how the values of personal and social responsibility were reflected through physical activity. They saw them through their own participation and by watching their adult leaders.

This is the way we did it. You may choose to—or need to—proceed differently, depending on your leadership position, setting, access to assistants who can help you, and other factors (see chapter 10 on problem-solving).

All of our programs introduce to the leaders effective teaching strategies that help them experience success. These strategies include thoughtful planning as well as "on-the-feet" teaching techniques. Having a grasp of these is not automatically gained with most leaders. Although a few leaders may have a reasonable grasp of teaching approaches, most young leaders will need guidance.

Cross-age Leadership represents the third stage of leadership development. Sometimes this stage is referred to as "cross-age teaching," although our kids like the term leader since they have already taught others their own age as described in stages one and two (chapters 5 and 6). Stage three leadership experiences are for those students who are ready and able to teach younger kids not only sport skills but also TPSR values. Consequently, this stage marks the beginning of developing leadership qualities that influence others to be responsible, caring, and compassionate human beings. There is also a fundamental shift in the way young people view themselves as a leader. They now begin to feel connected to a program they own (e.g., Youth Leader Corps)—a program that is mutually beneficial for them and the younger kids with whom they work. Although still present, their self-interests and needs begin to take a back seat to a commitment to help younger kids—they want to develop a positive relationship with them (Martinek, Schilling, & Hellison, 2006).

At this stage, progression and long-term planning, where leaders plan units of instruction over multiple lessons, are now required. Each lesson is built upon the previous one in order to accommodate a variety of skill and readiness levels of the children for whom they will be responsible. Along with planning, the pedagogy of organizing a class, observing what's going on, and communicating clearly are introduced.

By providing a sport program to other kids from the community, the concept of *service learning* is also introduced during this stage. Service learning is based on the assumption that young people (even our leaders) have a desire to be helpful to others (Hellison et al., 2007). Schools, universities, youth agencies, and churches all provide a variety of service opportunities to its members. Projects that engage young people in working with the homeless, beautifying parks and highways, building homes for Habitat for Humanity, and mentoring in school programs are just a few of the many ways these outside agencies try to instill the spirit of service in others. Unfortunately, many of our leaders have not had these opportunities, thus making this service learning experience a starting point to serve others and their community. Later, widening service opportunities will be part of the youth leader's program agenda.

Approaches to Cross-age Leadership

Cross-age leading programs can also be organized several ways. The approach you select will be based on what you feel is the best fit for your leaders. Their readiness and past experience will weigh in here. Two ways that have worked for us are assisting in a lesson and teaching in small and large groups (Hellison, 2003).

Assisting in a Lesson

This approach has been frequently used with "first time" leaders who are not quite sure of themselves. Here you can pair leaders to teach lessons to younger children where one of the leaders teaches, let's say a running tag game with some of the kids while the other is working with others on stretching exercises. Sometimes you may want the leader to work with an individual child who needs special assistance, or monitor a game or small group practice. Or you may have the leader watch you teach first. They can watch the way you organize and monitor an activity, give feedback, and conduct the closing reflection activity. Later on the leader takes over.

Teaching a Small and Large Group

With these approaches, each leader teaches with the same group for an entire lesson. Station work can use small group teaching by letting the leaders stay with their home group for the entire time. In large group teaching, some leaders may be able to handle the challenges of teaching an entire lesson to the whole group of children—they become like you! Over our years we have found that some leaders are capable of doing this. Of course, careful planning is needed here and usually this method is relegated to those leaders who are more experienced and confident.

What It Takes

Six core elements should be used to insure success of any cross-age leadership program. They are: (1) community connections with outside agencies that can supply younger children with whom to work, (2) a routine for leaders and participants to follow, (3) orientation and training to prepare the leaders for their new role, (4) teaching opportunities for leaders, (5) reflection and discussion, and (6) recognition and celebration (Hellison et al., 2000).

Community Connections

An important starting point is to identify and contact agencies that are willing to supply children for your leaders to teach. Of course, many of you may have kids readily accessible for your leadership program.

For example, if you work at a youth agency such as a Boys and Girls Club or a YMCA or teach PE at a K-8 school, younger kids will be available. Kim Berg, an elementary PE teacher, ran a "Breakfast Club" before school began and had middle school leaders work with selected elementary students who were struggling in the classroom.

For those who do not have an immediate source, connections and arrangements need to be made to either have kids come to your site or for you to gain access to the host site. For example, the Greensboro program is a campus-based program where children are transported to campus from outside agencies (i.e., schools and Head Start centers, child day care centers, local schools and Boys and Girls Clubs). Transportation, scheduling, selection of kids, and distance are important considerations when tapping into these outside resources.

Dave Walsh offers three important strategies that can help facilitate positive community connections (Walsh, 2002). First, you need to identify a contact person at the site. This person should be one who has direct contact with other staff and the youths. This person will help recruit kids, arrange transportation (if needed), inform other staff about the program, and even help in the evaluation process. Second, determine the age, gender, and number of kids that will be provided. Also, be sure that you get parents' names and phone numbers for emergency situations. And third, talk to the youths about the program, their commitment to it, and your role. Most will not have a clue about what the program is about or what your expectations for them will be. This meeting can take place at the site during- or after-operation hours.

This list of strategies to get younger kids involved in a cross-age leadership program can be daunting if you work alone and have a hundred other things to do. One of us runs a cross-age program very similar to what has been described. The other, who has less support and more of a "wing-it" style, has found nearby programs for younger kids with adult leaders willing to accommodate some kind of cross-age leadership program. If he gets approval, he tells his young leaders to take public transportation and be ready to "hit the ground running" when they arrive at the younger kids' site. Admittedly, this approach often looks pretty chaotic at first, but an hour every day devoted to post-leadership reflection by the youth leaders (led by the adult leader) gradually develops a routine with the young kids that, for the most part, works. A strength of this approach is that the youth leaders learn from the ground up about how to do this work. A weakness, as one graduate student observing the program put it, is that

"You [the adult leader] just throw them in there!" How does the adult leader respond to that?

Program Routine

There may be many ways to organize your leadership sessions. Regardless of the approach you decide to take, it is important to establish some routine that will be sustained throughout your program. The routine should be explained during the orientation meeting. This will help set the right tone for your leaders and the children with whom they work. Both of us have followed a similar routine through the years although there may be slight variations between them. Here is the routine our programs usually follow:

After the children enter the gym, they warm up by choosing a skill (e.g., volleying, passing, playing catch) and practice on their own or with a youth leader. During the first session, the children will be divided into smaller groups (six to eight) and assigned to a youth leader as a "home group." They will remain in that group for the remainder of the semester. Next, the adult leader calls the participants, staff, and youth leaders into a circle, reminds them of the daily goal(s) (e.g., trying your best), and sends them to their home stations. Later, the adult leader may assign one of the leaders to take on the responsibility of starting the program.

After five to seven minutes of instruction, the home groups rotate to another leader (station) who teaches them a different lesson while focusing on the daily goal(s). Each lesson is concluded with a "reflection" session. The youth leader reviews the skill and subsequently asks the children to reflect on their performance and their ability to work on the goal(s).

When leaders are paired together several options are available. One option is to have one leader teach the activity portion of the lesson and the other run the small group reflection sessions. Another option is to have one leader teach a skill (e.g., basketball dribbling) to half the group and the other teach defensive footwork to the other half. A third option, one that is most often used by leaders, is to switch roles with each rotation—one teaches and the other assists.

When the groups have rotated to all stations, they return to their "home-base" leader for final reflection. Then the groups come together with the program adult leader for large group discussion followed by dismissal.

After the kids have left, the adult leader, assistants, and youth leaders meet to talk about how things went and what things need to be worked on for the next session. Leaders then go off on their own (with the assistant) to do self- and assistant evaluations and to plan for next week's session.

Many of these ideas require assistants to help the adult leader as well as other support structures. As noted above, one of us has attempted to do cross-age leadership with fewer resources, and some adult leaders have even fewer resources and other issues in trying to put such a program into practice. The rule of thumb is to come as close as you can to the ideal structure and format for conducting a cross-age leadership program. Sometimes it won't be very close, but kids can still benefit from a more stripped down version.

Orientation and Training

Orientation and training helps the leaders make the transition from being a participant in a sport club to being a leader of one. This is a big role change for them and may require ample opportunity to prepare for it. In a sense, some of the training and orientation has taken place because of the leaders' previous membership in their TPSR sport club. They were able to see how the values of personal and social responsibility were reflected through physical activity and by watching you. Some were also able to step up and take on beginning leadership roles. On the other hand, it would be a big mistake to assume that all leaders have a complete grasp of ways to effectively plan, organize, teach, and direct small group discussion, as well as self-reflect and evaluate. And there will be some leaders who do not have previous club experience with TPSR. So preparing them will be of even greater importance. In either case, guidance from you will be needed.

Orientation and training programs vary across different programs. In Chicago, for example, Don and his assistants use an "on the spot" training approach. That is, kids are immediately placed into a cross-age leadership role where ample time is given to evaluate each session and prepare for the next. He has also used peer coaching in his middle school coaching clubs. The club becomes the training ground for his middle school kids. While Don has fewer resources than Tom, you may have fewer still, for example, no assistants. Once again, the rule of thumb is to get as close as you can.

Greensboro's Youth Leader Corps program includes two days of training with each lasting about 60 minutes. On the first day, the adult leader meets with the youth leaders and assistants to review the goals and expectations of the program. The assistants are usually undergraduate and graduate students from the university. Assistants provide

Stage 3: Cross-age Leadership 81

valuable support by guiding the leader in planning and teaching their lesson. If you have assistants, it is not a bad idea to have a separate meeting with them prior to the first with everyone. This provides an opportunity to have a candid discussion about their role and the importance of being committed to the goals of the program. Assistants can also be reminded that their job is to assist—not teach. They often have an innate urge to want to take over for a leader who may be floundering. This "rescue mentality" needs to be left at the doorstep. Jumping in only subverts the leader's role and diminishes self confidence.

The major portion of the first session covers what we call the "Four Bs" of leadership. Each "B" represents a focal point for the preparation and teaching of a lesson. The first B means "be ready." That is, having the lesson plan, teaching area, and "mind" ready before kids arrive is a must. This is often a big challenge for many of the leaders who bring in all kinds of issues from school and home experiences.

The second B means "be enthused." Youth leaders need to show kids that they are excited about being with them and really care about their learning. It is a good idea to remind them that a lousy attitude will quickly rub off on their kids. This is extremely important because leaders will vacillate in their willingness to take on the responsibilities of leading others. A good example of this was when one of our leaders, Tina, had her group running around while she had her head phones on listening to a CD. When asked by her assistant what was up, she said that her kids were uptight and needed to let off steam for a couple of minutes.

"Be with it," is the third B. This phrase is borrowed from Jacob Kounin's concept called "withitness" (Kounin, 1970) and underscores the importance of monitoring how the children are interacting with one another and how they are learning. Observing, which is a difficult but important teaching skill, comes into play here. Knowing what to look for, where to stand, and when to give feedback are some of the ally skills necessary for effective observation.

The final B stands for "be a role model." We always tell our leaders to never underestimate the influence they have by being a responsible leader. We remind them that kids not only look to leaders for guidance, but they watch how they interact with other leaders and how they value their leadership role. In essence, what children see and hear will be viewed as "the norm" for the program.

Each leader is also given a notebook which serves as a personal place for journaling, lesson planning, and evaluation. Samples of the content of the notebook are provided in appendix 1.

The session is concluded by asking leaders if they want the program to focus on only one sport (e.g., basketball) or multiple sports. Typically, they want to teach an activity with which they are familiar and therefore prefer a multiple sports format. In Don's Chicago program a single sport is taught (usually basketball), since it is central to both leaders and younger kids' lives (for better or worse). Kids provide their preference on an index card and are subsequently matched according to their sport preference. Assistants are then assigned to the paired leaders.

The second day of orientation and training helps the leaders get comfortable with their new role as leaders. We have found that even if you have already had your leaders experience peer teaching (e.g., coaching clubs) the transition from club-participant to adult-leader/teacher of young children can be a formidable one, for some more than others.

Leaders and assistants meet in the gym and review the program goals and routine. Here, the adult leader runs a mini-club session that includes leadership awareness strategies (peer teaching and coaching). Both the leaders and assistants participate with the purpose of reviewing leadership roles. During the session the leaders act as participants. The assistants are assigned to run a station with the leaders working in small groups rotating from station to station. This gives the leaders an idea of how the program will run and how reflection sessions are conducted. Afterward, the entire group meets to go over any issues that came up during the session. Finally, a meeting between the leaders and their assistants takes place to plan for the first day of the program. What to teach and who will teach it (in the case of paired leaders) are typically the focal points of this meeting. The lesson plan is then entered in the planning book by each leader—ready for the first lesson that lies ahead.

Opportunities to Lead

Earlier we described various teaching opportunities that are provided the youth leaders. These opportunities are the keys to eventually turning young people into caring and compassionate leaders. Beyond guiding the leaders through their teaching experiences, we have found that several things must occur in order to have them produce a caring and compassionate leader. First, the leaders need to know something about the sport they are teaching. That's one of the reasons that basketball in Chicago's program is usually taught. Other sports can be included and giving kids choices will help here. Kids will typically choose an activity with which they are most familiar or are skillful in.

Second, you should "size up" the leaders and see how much responsibility they can handle...even at this more advanced stage of leadership development. Some leaders will "shine" in their leadership role one day and fall flat on their face the next. The main culprits for this instability are frequently found in the challenges they face outside of the program (e.g., home and school circumstances). For example, one of our middle school leaders, Nicole, had been an excellent leader in our program. Although she had some initial struggles, her ability to connect to kids and teach the TPSR values to younger children was always "right on." Due to problems occurring at home, she suddenly became problematic for the program and it was a challenge to get her back on track. She was not focused on her leadership responsibilities and began to distract the other leaders. We found ourselves back peddling and searching for ways to get Nicole's previous leadership qualities to return.

Third, leaders need to conduct their own awareness talks. This is one of the most difficult tasks for them (some adult leaders as well). There are some things that you can do to help your leaders overcome this hurdle. One thing that Don has the leaders do is to have them take turns conducting the awareness talk with the large group at the end of a program session. They can volunteer for these assignments, or you can invite them to take over from time to time. Then you can have them run their awareness talks with their small groups (after each rotation).

Another approach, especially with leaders who are not very talkative, is to try something like one of our leaders, Rayshawn Page, did. He created his own rating card for his group members to fill out at the end of each lesson so they could assess their performance—thanks Rayshawn (see figure 7.1).

Lastly, leaders need to eventually create lessons that impart the virtues of being caring and compassionate to others. Alfie Kohn (2006) argues that teaching is not just merely producing good learners. Rather, it is about producing good people. Accomplishing such a goal requires our leaders to revisit some of their stage two experiences. For example, inclusiveness is reinforced by organizing small-sided games with "all-touch" and "soft defense" rules so the younger children become responsive to the individual differences of their teammates. A second way is teaching with compassion. Here, once again, leaders are encouraged to respond to those children who are struggling emotionally or physically. Begin looking for indicators like one-on-one guidance for those in need, being attentive, letting children express their opinions,

Basketball Camp

CAMPER THOUGHTS

How well did you work with others today?

How hard did you try at the activities—
Did you give your very best?

How did you work on your own?

How well did you help others?

Comments (things you did well or need to work on):

Figure 7.1 Give up the rock

and giving personal choices. These types of responses from your leaders will serve as emerging signs of compassionate leadership.

Reflection

As within the previous stages of leadership development, personal reflection should be an integral part of the cross-age leadership experience. Reflection means having the leaders ask questions such as "What am I doing?" "Why am I doing it?" "What am I learning?" and "How are the kids responding?"

Opportunities for reflection may be structured or unstructured. They can involve thinking, writing, and talking about what they did, saw, and felt during their lesson. One way to promote reflection is to give written and oral feedback to the leaders following a lesson. This gives them something for them to think about and respond to. Observing and meeting with a couple of leaders each session works best. Helping the leaders give clear directions, reminding them to be ready to lead, showing them how to arrange equipment and handle discipline problems, and fostering responsible behaviors and attitudes will give them valuable things to reflect upon. A second way is to have assistants facilitate the reflection process. In Tom's programs each leader is assigned an adult assistant (usually an undergraduate or graduate student). The assistant meets with the leader to discuss the lesson with the leader. Discussion can center on numerous aspects of the experience which gives the leader something to think about for the next lesson. If you do not have assistants, peer coaching can be used. This works especially well when you have leaders working in pairs. Guidance is needed here. Nick Cutforth used his training sessions to help the peer coach in this process.

Youth leaders can also keep a personal journal. You can have them write on an index card or in a notebook about their session: what things went well, what things didn't. The Greensboro leaders, for example, have a section in their planning book where they rate their lesson and make comments (see appendix 1).

Keep in mind that the depth of their written work will vary considerably. Some leaders will write more than others and show surprising insights in their leadership development. The important point here is that by writing down their thoughts (as brief as some may be) a leader will more likely become aware of their growth as a leader. Reading journals will take worthwhile time. However, if it is too much for you, choose another approach.

Group meetings always are a great way to ensure personal reflection. Adult leaders and assistants can serve as facilitators and "sounding boards" for the leaders. An important benefit gained from group reflection is that leaders can respond to each others' comments and draw some insight as to how their experience compared to others. In some cases, leaders can even offer suggestions for improvement to those who are having difficulty. Your job as a facilitator is to keep the things positive and constructive. Put downs need to be averted; they can only lead to a negative experience for all.

One simple approach to group reflection is to address each of the Four Bs separately by having the leaders point their thumbs up, sideways, or down for each of the Bs. For example, the question, "How well were you planned for your lesson today?" asks leaders to point their thumb up if they were well prepared, thumbs sideways if they were somewhat prepared, or thumbs down if they were not prepared at all. Before you go on to the next B be sure to look around to make sure each leader's thumb is indicating their response to the question. This will give you an idea of how the entire group of leaders saw themselves in relation to that particular B. Sometimes just a simple raising of the hand can be used in the evaluation process. One challenging question that we have used at the end of the group meetings as a lead-up to stage 4 leadership is: "How were you able to apply any of the Bs outside of the program?"

Your choice of reflection opportunities will depend on which one you feel will foster a strong sense of personal control and community among the leaders. Self-reflection will increase the probability of getting your leaders to be autonomous problem solvers. Thus, a spirit of stepping up and taking chances to help others can be ignited within each leader.

Celebration

Our leaders are seldom (if ever) recognized at end-of-the-year school award ceremonies. This is why we think it is so important to acknowledge their service achievement in our leadership programs. It is a chance to celebrate each leader's unique contribution to the program and others.

There are several ways of celebrating. Don always throws an end-of-the-year pizza party for his leaders. He acknowledges each leader's accomplishments and gives him or her a personal letter of recognition, clothing donated by a sporting good company, a gift certificate, and trip to a sporting goods store to cash the certificate in, and/or a free pass to the university recreation center. Don's leaders even enjoyed the visibility gained from attention received in the university paper, alumni magazine, and on a local television station.

Like Don, Tom's youth leaders have a dinner at the university with staff and leaders. In some instances, a community leader has been a special speaker at the occasion. Local news and media coverage have also highlighted the leaders' work. Tom also gives each leader a letter of thanks for their work along with some things to think about for the next year. One year (thanks to a suggestion by Nick Cutforth) Adidas donated shoes and warm up outfits. Some leaders even spoke about their leadership experiences at statewide profession meetings.

The great artist Michelangelo once said that inside every block of stone or marble dwells a beautiful statue; one need only remove the excess material to reveal the work of art within (from Rosamund and Benjamin Zander's *The Art of Possibility*). In a sense, the moment of celebration is a time where the negative baggage so often shouldered by our leaders is replaced with a sense of accomplishment and an awareness of their special qualities. It is our wish that such recognition by you will nudge your leaders closer to a fuller realization of their leadership capabilities.

Insights and Take-aways

Former L.A. gang member, Luis Rodriguez, proclaims that a culture is made around what we do with young people (Rodriguez, 2001). Creating the right culture that stimulates leaders' sense of responsibility to lead (and care for) younger children will require persistent guidance on your part. It will also absorb a considerable amount of energy from you—both physical and emotional. Personnel commitment, time to think and plan, and administrative and colleague support need to be there as you wade through the challenges facing you.

In this chapter are ideas that have worked for us in facing these challenges. At the same time, we fully realize you will tweak these ideas in ways to fit your situation. And, we also know that you will have your own approaches to add to the cross-age leadership experience. But, whatever you decide to do, here are some things from this chapter to take with you:

- A range of Stage 3 learning experiences are available, as we have shown. Your job is to apply them in a way that works for you.
- Operating at this stage of leadership is not a permanent thing! Be prepared for the "ups" and "downs" as leaders experience this new level of leadership responsibility. One moment leaders may seem to "shine" and the next they digress to earlier stages of leadership readiness.
- Effectively engaging young leaders in service learning work will depend on program quality. Ironing out all the logistical kinks (e.g., space, transportation, scheduling) will be needed to insure the quality you seek in your program.
- Look for shifts in the way your leaders perceive their role. Reprioritizing needs so that personal ones become secondary to those of the children with whom they work is what you are looking for. This will be an important indicator of readiness to move to the next stage of leadership (Self-actualized Leadership).

8

Stage Four: Self-actualized Leadership

There are two great moments in a person's life. The first is when you are born. The second is when you discover why you were born.

—Unknown

It was late afternoon in October when Tom received an unexpected phone call from Kevin, a former youth leader. Kevin was calling from an air force base in South Dakota. He had just returned from a tour in Iraq and would be stationed at the base for several months. Although he had received occasional emails from Kevin during his military tour, Tom had not heard from Kevin for several months since his last email. The call was a pleasant surprise.

Kevin started with Tom as a sixth grader in the Project Effort Sport Club and continued in the Youth Leader Corps program throughout high school. Raised by his mom in one of Greensboro's public housing complexes, Kevin managed to do well throughout school. Kevin's leadership skills were above many of his peer leaders and he showed great promise to go on to college. Spurred on by a summer internship at a local website business, Kevin became particularly interested in computer technology.

Then one day Kevin told Tom that he did not want to go college. Rather, he wanted to enlist in the air force. Although this was somewhat disappointing, Tom knew that this was what Kevin wanted to do—it was his choice. Kevin was assigned the job of a weapons technician—something that matched his career interests and skills.

The voice over the phone sounded excited. After exchanging "hellos" and "how's it going" Kevin explained why he really called. He told Tom that he was assigned to direct a youth program on his base and wanted to get ideas about getting started. He said, "I want to run a program like Project Effort—the kids here need it! Can you send me any material that can get me started?" Kevin's request was truly a "shot in the arm" for Tom and bolstered his belief that young leaders are capable of generating new interest and energy in parts of their lives—beyond those in the leadership program.

Stage Four, *Self-actualized Leadership*, focuses on a small, but important area of one's life. This means that a young leader acquires the energy, resources, and guidance to pursue a personal vision. In a sense, it is what psychologist Erik Erikson once described as "identity formation" where new and different choices are made (Erikson, 1994). The new choices have more to do with purpose and, perhaps, the common good of others (Damon, 2008). And, these choices are governed, to certain extent, by the leadership values and skills acquired in their early stages of leadership development.

So how will you know if a leader has advanced to the self-actualized stage? Initial signs of this kind of advancement will vary from leader to leader. One indicator is an increase in the leader's willingness to be more reflective of his or her leadership role. Formed by past successes and failures in teaching others, they begin to learn more about themselves and how the role of being a leader fits into a bigger picture—their future. Another sign is the leader's spontaneous effort to step out and help other leaders—even guide them through challenging moments. Finally, reciprocal learning is evident (Martinek, Schilling, & Hellison, 2006). That is, youth leaders begin to see (and internalize) their role as a leader beyond just teaching others.

For some leaders, the advancement to this stage is a huge leap from peer and cross-age teaching. And for some, the leap may be too far. The extent to which you, as an adult leader, view the readiness of youth to venture into this next stage will depend on a couple of things. One is their growth throughout the previous stages of leadership development. There will be no benefit gained by pushing kids to this level of leadership if they were unable to be responsible club participants and leaders. Even some of the leaders who have been with us seven and eight years still struggle to advance through the previous stages.

Second, a level of courage to apply their leadership skills beyond the confines of the gym walls or playground fences becomes evident. Although your guidance should continue (something we will discuss later in this chapter), vague and sometimes foreboding anxiety will be created when extending this leadership role to broader community contexts.

A leader's personal sense of the "best fit" is a third thing to consider. This will come into play in choosing stage four experiences. Self-awareness of capabilities and limitations will dictate what leaders are willing to take on. Like, Kevin, many are capable of making the right choice, for the right reason. College was not something Kevin wanted. He saw his strength as having knowledge in computer technology and saw the Air Force as a vehicle for applying his computer skills—a perfect fit!

Fostering Self-actualized Leadership

As we just noted, the focus of the fourth stage of leadership development now turns inward. For us, this is the highest level of leadership in that competencies in a young person's life are within areas and activities that have personal importance. This creates a unique advantage for young leaders. It solidifies their identity in an adolescent world and it provides them with a natural support system (Kouzes & Posner, 2008; van Linden & Fertman, 1998). We must also be mindful that the path each leader takes will be formed by a personal choice. Kevin is a good example of a leader who apparently developed into a strong leader and acquired a set of skills that positioned him to make a career choice of his own. But the path is not always direct, and trying to predict the end result will only cause frustration. Your job, and ours, is to create (and share) those experiences that support their aspirations and, perhaps, dreams.

An important factor in widening the vision of leadership and possible futures is to connect kids to broader spectrum of opportunities in their community. We have found that there are four sources that serve to support community engagement for leaders who reach this stage of leadership development. They are as follows: (1) institutions of higher learning, (2) career clubs, (3) community service, and (4) internships.

Institutions of Higher Learning

Many leaders see college as beyond their reach—even at this developmental stage. In fact, there will be those who have never stepped foot on a university campus. Some cross-age teaching programs (see chapter 7) allow leaders to work with other children in a university setting. Bringing leaders on a campus exposes them to an academic environment. These types of experiences can increase the leaders' comfort in the university setting—perhaps raising aspirations to go on to college

(Cutforth & Puckett, 1999). Thus, we are suggesting that the leaders' familiarity with the university may be a catalyst to pursue a post-secondary interests.

In chapter 7 we described two programs where leaders teach on a university campus (i.e., Greensboro's Youth Leader Corps and Chicago's Summer Apprentice Teaching Program). While their focus is on developing leadership skills through cross-age teaching opportunities, being on a university campus has sparked post-secondary interests in some of our leaders. In the Chicago program, Don further fueled the leaders' interests by adding the *Neighborhood Scholar Program*. This program provides an incentive for leaders to continue their education beyond high school. Funding by Nike along with guidance from the Chicago Workforce Development Partnership supported postsecondary education at UIC, another four-year institution, a community college, or a trade school. Even job placement could be provided in special cases.

In Greensboro, the youth leaders are allowed to have dinner at the university cafeteria with the staff (after each program session), further exposing them to the university culture. When funding is available, small stipends have been paid to the leaders for their work in the program. Business and professional leaders have also been invited to discuss career and leadership opportunities with the leaders. Some of the professional leaders, in fact, came from underserved neighborhoods and therefore became role models for the leaders.

For many of you, running a campus-based program is not possible. However, a visit to a campus with your leaders may be sufficient. In Denver, Nick Cutforth's school-based program does this. Each year his youth leaders visit the university. Professors, undergraduates, and graduate students would talk to the youth leaders about campus life, academic demands, and daily routines. This also helps them see the connection of doing well in school and living successful and personally meaningful lives (Hellison et al., 2000).

Career Clubs

Dave Walsh (2008) empowered students to explore their possible futures using an innovative approach to the TPSR model. Based on Markus and Nurius' theory (Markus & Nurius, 1986) of possible selves, Dave developed a career club with a group of Chicago middle school students who were previous participants in a TPSR Coaching Club (see chapter 5). The career club was an extension of the coaching

Stage 4: Self-actualized Leadership 93

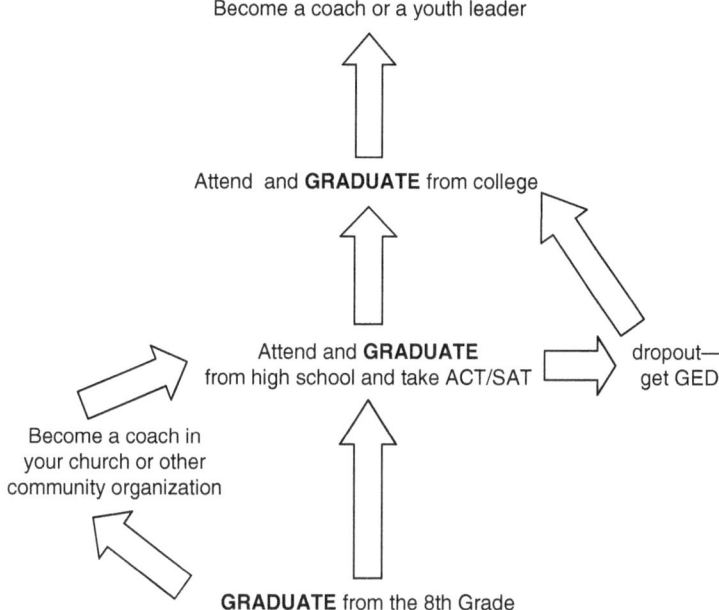

Figure 8.1 Career path for the coaching club

club in that the participants were responsible for coaching younger kids. The aim of the program was to develop an awareness of what it takes to become a successful coach or youth worker. To do this, he began by helping his participants think about coaching as a career, and then broadened this perspective to career exploration with emphasis on the 'procedural knowledge' needed to take appropriate steps toward fulfilling this career aspiration (see figure 8.1).

Similar strategies that were previously used in TPSR programs (i.e., group discussions, reflection and journal writing, and teaching opportunities) were employed to increase the club member's awareness of what it takes to become a successful youth worker and coach. A "Career Club Workbook" included a form to self-evaluate (see table 8.1) and set goals for their chosen career, whether it was youth worker, coach, or a career not related to sport (being a police officer or lawyer had several takers).

The Career Club provided a realistic, hands-on approach to some of the difficulties of 'making it' in the real world and the need for problem-solving as well as organizational and verbal skills. It also served as an excellent way to exploit the readiness of those leaders

Table 8.1 Career club workbook evaluation form

Date:	Skill Knowledge	Planning	Verbal
You goal:	High Okay Low	High Okay Low	High Okay Low
How did you goal go?	High	Okay	Low
Comment:			

Answer one of the following questions:
1) What did you learn about your coaching skills?
2) What are some of the coaching qualities that make you a good coach?
3) Has today's experience helped push you toward or away from thinking about a coaching career?
4) What do you hope to become in the future?
5) What are you afraid to become in the future?
6) Can the coaching skills that you are learning transfer to other careers? If so, how?
7) Are you changing in any ways that will help your possible future?

who see themselves in some leadership capacity in the future. But "readiness" is a key to the success of such programs. By Dave's own admission (Walsh 2008, p. 220), young middle school students may not respond as well as their older high school counterparts who are closer to pursuing their future career goals.

Community Service

Communities, by and large, have strong interests in fostering good citizenship among their young people. Therefore, opportunities for doing service work are abundant. Both of us feel that community service is a critical step forward in getting leaders to embrace the importance of community engagement. This is especially relevant for the leaders with whom we work. Unfortunately, schools serving low income students are less likely to engage in service activities (Scales & Roehlkepartain, 2004). Fortunately, churches, youth agencies, and civic groups provide alternative service segues for your leaders. By collaborating with these outside agencies you create a win-win situation. That is, asset building is realized by both the young leaders and these community partners (Benson, 2006).

Both of us have been able to tap into some of these community resources. Don had his high school leaders provide instructional assistance in the National Youth Sport Program (NYSP) during the summer.

NYSP was a national program funded by the NCAA that provides an array of activities for underserved kids. The leaders became part of NYSP instructional staff and added a values-based instruction component to NYSP's program agenda. Having the leaders assist also helped to decrease the teacher-child ratio for the NYSP teaching staff.

Similarly, Tom's leaders have become part of the local Boys and Girls Club in Greensboro. Each week leaders travel to a nearby Boys and Girls Club Center to provide sport and arts and craft instruction to the club's younger children. In some cases special events (i.e., car wash, talent night) have been planned together with the leaders and Boys and Girls Club staff.

More recently, Greensboro's leaders established a shelter for homeless families on UNCG's campus. This new initiative was part of a collaborative arrangement with UNCG's Campus Ministry, who supplied the building and kitchen space, and a local outreach group whose mission was to locate space and human support for homeless families in Greensboro. This initiative extended the scope of service work of the leaders beyond just teaching physical activity. Rather, it gave them responsibilities of providing bedding, breakfast and dinner, conversation with the guest families, and recreational time with their children. An important responsibility of the adult leaders was to help the leaders resist the tendency to interpret their roles as charitable ones. Instead, *supportive engagement* was the hallmark of this type of community service.

Internship Programs

Internships for the self-actualized leader integrate real work experience with his or her leadership skills. In general, internships have typically been part of vocational training programs that are either nested in secondary schools (career enrichment classes) or in community colleges. Unfortunately, most large schools (and even some community colleges) tend to resist internships. They can't imagine setting up internships for 2000 of their students. That's why your small group of leaders (and small alternative schools) will work well. In addition, school internship programs often require academic prerequisites that many underserved kids can't or don't want to acquire. With such a thrust toward testing and meeting academic standards, schools often make students feel that if you can't learn to convert fractions or read Dickens, you will never get a job *and* make a living. Quincy Howe, author of *Under Running Laughter*, believes (as we do) that there needs to be a fine line continually drawn and redrawn between the work kids need but hate and the more agreeable work that can address their limitations (Howe, 1991).

Clearly, vocational training would be strong component in any program. For example, each year in the city of Greensboro, over 25,000 jobs open up that do not require a college diploma (North Carolina Employment Security Commission Report, 2007). These are not just menial jobs, but skilled jobs like machine tool operators, roofers, stone cutters, landscapers, photographers, and automotive technicians, cosmetologists, office administrators, truck drivers, and file clerks. Professional training and job placement support for these positions will not only nourish a student's self respect but may set the stage for follow up remediation in academic subjects (Howe, 1991).

Most of our internships have taken place during the summer since this is the time when flexible scheduling seems to be most abundant. In Greensboro's Youth Leader Corps, summer internships were offered to those leaders who were interested in having one. Based on their personal preference we were able to set up four sites for our leaders: (a) an automotive service business, (b) a Web site design company, (c) a law office, and (d) a fire department. It is important to note, however, that with careful jostling of school and workplace schedules internships can also take place during the school year.

We have also found that some preliminary preparation is helpful. Given your situation, you may want to do this in a way that best interfaces with available resources, personal scheduling, and site personnel availability. We have found that four phases of preparation seem to work best for us. The first phase identifies internship sites and supervisors in the community. This is where having community connections become important. Although it takes a little more time than email, personal contact always works best here. Once contact has been made, a confirmation letter is sent to each site member.

In the second phase an "advisory board" composed of site personnel, university staff, and interns is formed. The advisory board develops guidelines for maximizing the quality of the internship experiences. This is an important time to share ideas and to get a feel for each others' expectations for the internship experience.

The third phase includes a work session for the interns and the community partners. The session reviews the *basic requirements* for the internships. Attendance, record keeping, journaling, and money management skills need to be highlighted during this time. In addition, the importance of *developing generic job skills* needs to be addressed. Skills like self-presentation, attitude, communication,

Table 8.2 Internship journal card

Date:
Internship Site:
What kinds things did you do today?:
What did you learn from today's experience (about job and self)?:
Rate the day's experience:
All World _____   Good _____   Fair _____   Not so good _____
Rate your work performance today:
All World _____   Good _____   Fair _____   Not so good _____
Comments:

---

organization and time management, and teamwork should be emphasized. Knowledge about the specific product, technicalities, and policies and procedures of youth leaders' specific work sites is also an important aspect of the session's agenda.

The final phase includes the implementation of the internships. During the summer, each youth leader interns at a site for a specified number hours per week, typically for a six-week period. During the school year the hours will vary considerably according to workplace and leader schedules. As in other stage experiences, personal reflection is needed. Reflecting about the internship experience can take the form of a free-flowing discussion about each internship experience, or it can be a more formal process where interns fill out an "Internship Journal Card" after each session (see table 8.2). In addition, a culminating activity in Greensboro has been a celebration pizza party with the site personnel, university staff, and leaders. This is also a great time to discuss and evaluate the experiences.

A Word about Adult Roles

We want to underscore the important roles that adults play in stage four leadership development. Because your leaders may be active at a university, doing community service, involved with a career club, or participating in an internship, you will find that adults play numerous and important roles. They act as role models and mentors by setting examples, giving feedback, and providing emotional support. They also become valuable resources that not only provide ways of pursuing future interests but also ways of getting there. The potential for future action was evident when one of our veteran youth leaders, Derek, recently proclaimed that in a few years he is going to have Tom's job!

In a certain way, adults essentially become *partners* when they share their academic, recreational, and vocational experiences and expertise with their leaders. Leaders are able to see the fascination and commitment from adults for what they do. This was the case with one of Greensboro's site supervisors, George Durham.

George owns a small, but flourishing, automotive business in Greensboro. He is also president of the city's Black Business Owners Association. For the past several summers, George has been a great mentor for the youth leader interns. As a child, he was raised in public housing by several caretakers (a mom—when she was off drugs, grandmother, and close friends). He, like many kids in his neighborhood, was continually enticed to join gangs, peddle dope, and just get into trouble. One day he decided to join a program provided by his church that taught individuals about automotive care. The person running the program, also an automotive business owner, took special interest in George and let him work in his shop. Immediately, George was hooked with this type of work. He saw purpose to it and was enamored by the future possibility of having his own business. He finished high school, went to a community college to learn more about automotive technology, and...the rest is history.

George always attends our end of the year celebrations and shares his life story with our leaders. His message reinforces three simple principles: listen to people who want to help—don't blow them off, jump on every opportunity that comes your way, and give back to your neighborhood and community. Each year his message sparks energy and purpose for our youth leaders.

One last thought about adult roles in stage four leadership. Adults who work with your leaders in a community setting will probably face some personal challenges. We discuss these challenges when our advisory board meets. One of these challenges is to understand that adolescent leaders have a difficult time behaving consistently (even at the stage of leadership). Some are eager to work but may find that menial jobs (e.g., sweeping up, filing, answering phone calls, data entry) are not always what they expected. Adult frustration can quickly creep in when leaders delay work, have too many excuses, procrastinate, and waste time. They want to work, but not that kind of work! Matching the leader's professed beliefs and attitudes about work will be a slow process for the site supervisor. And reaching that point may become a frustrating and protracted process.

Another challenge is communication. Site supervisors will find that leaders have their own way of expressing things. When these expressions are viewed to be inappropriate it becomes troublesome for the site supervisor. Your training sessions will need to address this. Young leaders will sometimes be put off by thinking that any objection to using certain expressions is an indication of "attitude" and not of message content. Supervisors need to be aware of this so that work relationships do not become contentious.

A third challenge is to make sure that adults are "up front" with the leader about appearance and the work place. Wearing a "wife beater" t-shirt, or jeans hanging below the butt, or shirts with inappropriate sayings will not fit into the mainstream workplace. This can be difficult for the site supervisors since they don't want to offend or embarrass the young leaders. But having the intern know this early prevents problems from occurring later. For example, one of our leaders, Whitney, went to have an initial interview by a female site supervisor who was a lawyer. Whitney got all dressed up but wore a very tight blouse and very short skirt. The very first thing the lawyer pointed out was the "inappropriateness" of her outfit. In a respectful but poignant way she told Whitney: "If you dress that way, you will never be taken seriously as a woman lawyer!" This was a great, straightforward message, one that was taken to heart by Whitney.

A final challenge for adults is dealing with the leaders' behavior in a consistent way. Supporting leadership behavior is easy when the behavior is seen as favorable. But when the behavior is not favorable, it is difficult to see any benefits. Constructive feedback (versus destructive feedback) can also serve as a supportive response when the leader's behavior is not positive. This approach is also important when adult supervisors want leaders' opinions but decide afterward what to respond to and what to ignore. Doing this is worse than not asking for opinions at all. The value of the message is lessened and the leader is led to believe that he or she is not important.

Insights and Take-aways

Self-actualized leadership experiences are about opening windows and letting the future in. It's about planting seeds (even if they are the size of muster seeds!) that will hopefully germinate into broader and more powerful views of one's capabilities. By giving your leaders a vision for a possible future you will have put them in a better position to reach beyond what is, into what can be. But all the above experiences will not be the end point for them. You (and we) cannot predict what the result will be because leadership, even at this self-actualized stage, is an ongoing process. As you continue to find ways to trickle out (as we have) promising ways to raise a young person's hope for a better future, we would like you to keep the following in mind:

- Successful advancement to stage four will depend on your leaders' readiness and growth in the previous stages of leadership development. The appropriateness of the experience will also be a huge factor in acquiring meaning and purpose for your leaders.
- Community connections play an important role in this stage of leadership development. An array of service learning and vocational enrichment learning opportunities will be available in your community. With your guidance, these opportunities will engage leaders in meaningful service to their community.
- Adult roles must be realized during this stage of leadership development. This means that community partners (site supervisors) must be prepared for mentoring and supporting the young leaders as they work and learn in the mainstream of their community. A large part of what they learn will come from those adults guiding them through stage four learning experiences.
- Self-actualized leadership is an ongoing process. Total transformation can only take place when your leaders see them themselves as *true contributors* and *positive change agents* to their community and perhaps the world.

III

Making Leadership Work

9
Relationships with Leaders

Kids will remember what you said to them some of the time. And, they will remember what you did with them some of the time. But they will always remember how you made them feel.

—Unknown

Individual positive relationships with kids in the program are at the core of both TPSR and youth leadership. As we mentioned earlier, the three Rs of youth work are "relational, relational, relational." For that reason, we have devoted an entire chapter to it.

The five levels of responsibility represent skills and dispositions needed to become a youth leader. Level four in particular focuses directly on the qualities required of a youth leader. A student in the program cannot be a successful youth leader without respecting others' rights and feelings, being self-directed and cooperative, possessing the ability to be self-directed, and being caring, sensitive, and responsive in interactions with others. Our view of helping others does not include expectations of extrinsic rewards or being arrogant or judgmental. It also involves listening to peers, only offering help if it is wanted, and helping others to solve conflicts peacefully.

Who Is the Adult Leader?

Adopting (and adapting) the levels means not only teaching, but living and embodying them. As Nick Forsberg pointed out, it is a "way of being"—being respectful, being self-motivated and cooperative, being self-directed, and being a servant leader whose purpose is to serve others

(Komives, Lucas, & McMahon, 1998). In other words, the adult leader is a leadership role model, so that students can not only observe the levels of responsibility in practice, but experience them firsthand over time in a one-on-one relationship, We have learned that such relationships encourage students to integrate and apply these qualities more than any other single TPSR strategy. These relationships also come in handy when youth leaders need to be confronted before, during, or after the program for not doing their job, losing their temper, or making excuses for their missteps (see the relational problem-solving section later in this chapter for specific examples from our experiences). Further, learning from these bonds can spill over to their lives outside the gym and especially to becoming a role model for peers and younger kids.

Relational Qualities

To begin, we highlight some key qualities and skills to help program directors build positive relationships with youth leaders. Four fundamental relational qualities that are integral to TPSR will greatly facilitate relationships with youth leaders (see table 9.1).

Each Youth Leader Has His/Her Own Individuality and Identity

Despite dressing, talking, gesturing, and even walking in a similar way, each differs in very unique ways. Some are outgoing and some are very quiet. They come with their own personal baggage. Some respond to constructive criticism better than others. And, yes, programs range in their gender, race, and ethnicity makeup. Indeed, the term "sameness" becomes obsolete for these kids. But beyond all the labels placed on them one thing is certain: They want to be respected for who they are. This is an important starting point for discovering their strengths and talents as leaders.

Each Youth Leader Has Something to "Bring to the Table"

Sure, leaders will have deficiencies, but preoccupation with trying to fix them will assuredly keep a program director from discovering and

Table 9.1 Basic director–youth leader relationship qualities

Recognition and respect for a youth leader's individuality and identity.
Recognition and respect for a youth leader's strengths.
Recognition and respect for a youth leader's capacity to make good decisions.
Recognition and respect for a youth leader's voice.

enhancing their strengths. Think about it. Why would any kid who felt rejected and incomplete be willing to take chances to lead others? By focusing on the leader's strengths instead of deficiencies creates honest and open dialogue about issues that are critical to the developmental process. Youth leaders will be more willing to work on issues like conflict with others, slacking off on their leadership responsibilities, and so on.

Each Youth Leader Is Capable of Making Good Decisions

Earlier in this book we discussed the importance of power sharing in leadership programming. The "heart and soul" of the power-sharing process is the adult leader's willingness to allow his or her youth leaders to be decision makers. There will be many opportunities in the programs for youth leaders to decide what is best for them, their students, and the program itself. Although mistakes will be made, guidance will be tantamount to keeping youth leaders on track. The important thing is that opportunities must continue so the difference between good and bad decisions can be realized. It's the only way the learning curve for each leader can progress upwardly. The process is the important thing here.

Each Youth Leader also Teaches the Program Director

The voices of our leaders have taught us things that we never knew before. Their opinions have brought us closer to their own realities. This has allowed us to weigh them against our own views of life itself and what we think is really important. Someone once said that the best learning comes from people who are learning themselves. This adage certainly applies to both of us; that is, we have become better professors and teachers ourselves. And, we have learned that listening must be authentic; it's more than just showing that you care for them. It's about knowing more about a kid whose voice is typically not listened to, whose interests are a mystery to many, whose family is excluded from the mainstream, and whose feelings are ignored by their school. The key to developing this quality is not only listening to youth leaders but believing that they know things we don't.

Adult-leader Qualities

In addition to the above qualities, you will discover that other *personal attributes* help to fortify the bonds between you and your leaders. These are important to self examine because they not only define

Table 9.2 Other director–youth Leader relationship qualities

Genuineness and vulnerability
Intuition
Sense of humor and playful spirit
Cultural awareness

who you are but how they will impact your interactions with the leaders. Table 9.2 outlines these qualities.

Genuineness and Vulnerability

Genuineness has been implied in our discussion of the relationship qualities of a good adult leader. Phonies and role players (as opposed to role models) need not apply. Vulnerability is an important and often overlooked aspect of genuineness. Adults make mistakes just like kids do. Admitting one's mistakes may appear to weaken one's authority, but in our view, it just makes the adult leader more human and therefore more accessible.

Intuition

Rubin (1985) defined intuition in an educational setting as the ability to recognize clues in students' moods, attitudes, energy levels, openness to new ideas, and so on so the adult leader can adjust accordingly. It means sizing up the kids and the situation. It means asking "what can I get away with today?" What do you notice that changes your plan? What does their body language tell you? When do you need to be assertive? Do you back off? Do you invite someone to be a leader today? Paying attention to clues acknowledges an inconvenient truth: "The devil is in the details," something not covered in most lesson or program plans.

Following up on clues requires reflection-in-action (Schon, 1987) and can be facilitated by creating a solutions bank (Orlick, 1980). According to Schon, reflection-in-action consists of a creative in-the-moment response to the observed (or sensed) clues when the director has no prior knowledge to rely on. Creating a solutions bank augments the lesson or program plan by generating a list of possible moods, energy levels, attitudes, and other issues that might be encountered, followed by thinking through possible responses to these imaginary clues. The purpose is not necessarily to guess right about what might occur but to prepare for unexpected possibilities. More experienced youth leaders can also benefit from practice in looking for clues and responding to them.

Sense of Humor and a Playful Spirit

Responsible youth leadership is serious business and sometimes a lot to ask of kids. Lightening things up can ease some of the rocky times and "grease the skids" of a youth leadership agenda. One way of lightening things up is to simply have fun! If the adult leader has a playful spirit, it can become contagious. A manifestation of this is to *look like* you're having fun (thanks to Sarah Doolittle). Being upbeat in a gym or on the playing field should not be hard work for someone who enjoys sport and exercise.

A sense of humor helps too. This doesn't mean telling jokes. It's about seeing the humor in events as they unfold, interjecting fun into the process, and laughing at one's self ("if you can't fix it, laugh at it"). It's about being upbeat and actively engaged... and smiling often!

Cultural Awareness

We addressed this issue to some extent in our comments on respecting students' individuality. Learning about the neighborhood and culture(s) the kids live in is of paramount importance. Too often we get our information from "if it bleeds it leads" journalism and anything goes websites and blogs.

One way to learn is to practice "skillful inaction," a phrase coined by a new teacher in an Inuit village school as he described learning about foreign (to him) customs and rituals. Don't assume: Learn! That even goes for an adult leader with loads of experience but not in this neighborhood or culture. Another tip: Don't try to "go native" or be cool, for example, with the latest colloquial language or fancy handshake. Those things may develop naturally, but don't force them. In short, respect and learn from your youth leaders and their backgrounds.

Relational Time

Including relational time at the beginning of the daily format as described in chapter 4 gives the adult leader the opportunity to interact individually with as many students as possible before the organized part of the program begins. These mini-conferences are especially necessary for youth leaders. Do they have a specific plan? If so, what is it? Do they feel able to pull it off? Are they willing to be a servant leader? Plans can be modified, confidence bolstered, and their responsibility to others emphasized during this time. This is another opportunity to convey to youth leaders that they have strengths as well as things that need work, that each is a unique individual, that each has a voice that deserves a response, and that each has the capacity to make sound decisions.

Keep these conversations brief, sometimes just walking by a program leader to give a one sentence feedback regarding the last leadership experience or asking the youth leader if he is willing to be a youth leader today or if she has a plan and is ready to lead today. If someone one needs a little more preparation to lead, that can be done briefly as well. To some extent, the adult leader can plan for these little talks by deciding before the program begins what student assets, issues, or individual characteristics might be worth a small conversation.

Relational Problem-solving: Some Vignettes

Our leadership work with kids is grounded in TPSR and the leadership stages (chapters 5, 6, 7, and 8). These frameworks have served us well, but it is dangerous to pretend that this or any other framework can fully capture the idiosyncrasies and vicissitudes of human interaction in adult-student relationships. This point continues to remind us that relational work is a craft not a blueprint! To make such relationships more human, we include here some real-life examples of director-youth leader interactions in practice. (Pseudonyms are used to protect the identity of the youth leaders.)

All of the following examples are success stories from our perspective, but the role of the adult and youth leader varies, sometimes widely. Good relationships do not only require guidance and encouragement. They also require intuition (sizing up), confrontation, and backing off, depending on those involved and the situation. You will see all these things and more in these vignettes.

Antavis

Antavis was working with about ten kids when the action stopped. The adult leader went over, but Antavis waved him off with "I can handle this." A girl was crying, and a boy, staring at the floor, was clearly implicated. Antavis told the boy to apologize. He mumbled an apology, but the girl did not stop crying. So Antavis said "Say it like you mean it," and the boy tried again with the same result. Then

Antavis said "Tell her you won't do it again." He did, and she broke out in a big smile. The director gave a thumbs up and walked away. He had sized up the situation and wisely stayed out of it. Antavis used reflection-in-action to find a solution.

Roberta

Roberta had been a problem throughout her four years in the program, but she begged the adult leader to let her become a leader in a cross-age teaching program. The first day a little girl complained that as her coach, Roberta was hogging the ball. After the kids left, the director addressed the issue with Roberta. As usual, she looked away and refused to respond. The next day, another kid complained and the director told him to skip Roberta's station. Soon others added to the growing number of complaints. Each was told to skip her station. By the end of the session, Roberta was working with two kids instead of the usual eight to ten. Another one-on-one conversation with the adult leader replicated the first one (or perhaps the thousandth one over four years). The next day a mother and father of one of the little kids visited the program to lodge the same complaint. This time the adult leader took a hard line in his conversation with Roberta. She looked at the floor and pouted as he said "This isn't the NBA and it isn't your time to show off. If you can't show the kind of leadership we've worked on and you're capable of, here is your bus fare home." A very small voice replied, "I'll do it." And for the most part, she did.

Darrell

One adult leader shared a story about Darrell, one of his better youth leaders, who was in a gang and, as an eighth grader, ran young prostitutes while going to school. How could Darrell be chosen as a leader? The answer requires understanding these kids' experiences in the community and especially in their "street life." Darrell's exploits, if not typical, were also not very surprising (given the circumstances). If leadership held the potential to help these kids, they needed to experience it. Darrell's background and current activities influenced his day-to-day mood, requiring frequent one-on-one conferences and sometimes temporarily relieving him of his leadership responsibilities. As his adult leader commented, "It's part of the deal. Leadership promotes social development, but you have to hang in with these kids, and unlike fairy tales, they don't always end happily." In Darrell's case, however, it seemed to pay off. Although Darrell dropped out of school after the 8th grade, he showed up back at his old after-school club two years later, free of gang signs, dressed up and in high school out of his neighborhood.

Rashad

Rashad was in a TPSR-based basketball program from the third grade on for five years. He was a young and short but very talented basketball player. By the end of the third grade he could barely read and write which became apparent in his reflection time journal entries. As he got older, he was expected to take a leadership position as a player-coach, like others in the program. However, throughout the five years, Rashad never accepted the TPSR approach to sport. Instead, he let everyone know he was an NBA kind of guy—winning and self-promotion were most important and trash talk was part of the game. He and the adult leader had seemingly endless one-on-one meetings. Finally exasperated, the adult leader suggested he leave the program unless he could become the kind of leader expected and needed in the program. Rashad shook his head and left the gym. However, he showed no animosity, would routinely go out of his way to say hi to the adult leader, and even came to the program to observe. He later went on to be selected as an all state guard and received a scholarship to a major university basketball power. How he got through the academic requirements of high school and into a university remained a mystery (although not in a low income, minority, basketball-crazy community.

Melvin

The last story is about the sheer perseverance of one of the kids as well as an adult leader who took a chance. Melvin was a small skinny kid who came to the program with few (if any) athletic skills. He was picked on at the playground and on the street and got into several fights every week. Despite all this, he badly wanted to be a leader. He finally became an assistant leader (that is, ran a drill that the kids already knew how to do), and in a few years, as one of the oldest members of the program, the adult leader had to invite him to assume a leadership role. By that time, his skills had improved somewhat, and he lad learned to control his temper, resulting in fewer taunts. He still wasn't close to being a competent youth leader, but the director let him take his best shot. Two weeks later, the equivalent of a school superintendent and two principals from Ireland who wanted to see a leadership club in action showed up while he was coaching. He walked right over and invited them to play. They said they didn't know much about basketball, but Melvin just said "I'll teach you." He held a practice, taught the visitors a few of the basics, and they played along with the kids in the program. Afterward over coffee, the visitors couldn't talk enough about the experience and how wonderful Melvin was to them!

Insights and Take-aways

The issues surrounding successful youth leadership programming will be challenging, even for the most energetic and committed adult leader. Here some the main issues that need to considered:

- Perhaps the most daunting issue is the presence of the relationship with leaders in just about every aspect of a youth program, requiring that adult leaders be "on their toes" at all times. The relational needs of youth leaders only intensifies this issue. They need to be noticed and cared about just like other students, but they also need to be ready to lead. That means, among other things, receiving help in learning the necessary skills for planning and leading, getting feedback on their leadership experiences, and learning to respond to issues that arise among those they are trying to lead, such lack of attention, arguments, and defiance.
- Power-sharing can also be an issue. When is it the right time to give a student a leadership experience? What biases might prevent a director from inviting a student from becoming a youth leader? Often, biases originate in or are strengthened by a rocky director-student relationship. That is to be expected; after all, this is human work! But all adults who run programs need to be vigilant regarding favoritism and biases against particular students. As with other issues, keeping a self-reflection journal can help to control these biases.
- Because this is human work, no cut-and-dried solution to biases exists. Perhaps the best we can do is to know our biases (Myrdal, 1944), try to minimize their impact on kids, and pay attention to how we interact with kids in general and youth leaders in particular. It often helps to use a journal to keep track of one's relational strengths and weaknesses in specific situations. Over time the journal provides a snapshot of the extent of progress (or backsliding), providing feedback regarding what needs work and what strengths stand out.

10

Problem-solving in Youth Leadership

The road to success is always under construction.

—Lilly Tomlin

In writing about TPSR and the leadership stages, we try to be cognizant that the humanness of working with kids flattens out on paper. We use these frameworks because they provide programmatic guidance in such vital areas as purpose and direction and have stood the test of time in our work. But situational and plain old human factors have forced us to face problems unaccounted for by our frameworks. In fact, problem-solving is inextricably intertwined with youth work, a point driven home by two books about teaching kids, Joe McDonald's (1992) *Teaching; Making Sense of an Uncertain Craft* and Alan Tom's (1984) *Teaching as a Moral Craft*. The titles (and contents) of these two books explain why the fashionable educational goal of "going to scale" (i.e., duplicating a successful program at other sites) often fails (Coburn, 2003; Lytle, 2002).

Based on these factors as well as our own experiences, it behooves adult leaders of youth programs and, for our purposes, youth leadership programs to develop problem-solving skills. The first step is to identify the problem, a process called problem-setting (Lawson, 1984). This step is necessary, because if the problem itself is misdiagnosed, the problem-solving process will be derailed.

This chapter explores three sets of potential problems that adult leaders may face in implementing our approach to youth leadership:

- Building a TPSR foundation for one's leadership program.
- Addressing the unique variables that adult leaders face, such as different roles and contexts with different levels of support.

- Dealing on a daily basis with youth leaders' struggles, moods, and relational needs.

Building a TPSR Foundation

TPSR is not some theory dreamed up in an ivory tower. It has been adopted and adapted by many physical education teachers, as well as some youth workers and a few coaches in the United States and several other countries. Chapter 5 summarized the primary features of TPSR, which focus on kids learning to take more responsibility for their own development and well-being and for contributing to the development and well-being of others.

Because TPSR is foundational to developing the kind of youth leadership approach we advocate, it would be exceedingly difficult to start a leadership program with kids who have not learned how to work alone (independence, goal-setting) or with others (respect, cooperation, relational skills). Some teachers and youth workers unfamiliar with TPSR do emphasize being respectful, cooperative, and actively engaged, but fewer gradually shift their power to the kids, conduct frequent self-reflection sessions, or emphasize the relational aspects of individual and group interactions.

Since TPSR is stage one in the youth leadership process, an adult leader without a background in TPSR faces the problem of how to get started. A TPSR primer on getting started is available (Hellison, 2003, Chapter 9), but our point here is to problematize this issue and suggest a few possible solutions.

The approach both of us and some of our colleagues have used is to begin with a TPSR-based sports club as a "feeder" system to a youth leadership program. This can also be accomplished, at least to some extent, in a physical education class or even with a team in an organized sport program.

An alternative approach is to start a leadership club, remembering that in our view, all kids can be leaders. Those adult leaders who start the program with knowledge and perhaps experience in TPSR can begin with small leadership responsibilities, such as in the awareness talk asking one or two students to tell everyone what being a leader means, in the group meeting asking the kids to suggest ways of making the club better, and in reflection time by modeling honest self-evaluations to help others get the idea. Building on such opening activities, adult leaders can begin to encourage kids in the program to supervise a small group activity or run a drill for peers, or participate in peer teaching and coaching as described in stage two. During this process, all kids need to learn the fundamentals of leadership, whether or not they are ready to take on a small leadership responsibility. This works best by sharing brief leadership cues and giving specific feedback. In doing so, we try to stay within the "ten word rule" for adult leaders, which above all, means no long lectures! (When their attention begins to drift or they roll their eyes your talk is over!) Leadership cues could include taking charge, being positive, giving feedback, and so on.

Of course, throughout this process you may need to return to the TPSR fundamentals, sometimes frequently, especially respect for the rights and feelings of others, teamwork, effort, and goal-setting. Even in a leadership program, backsliding occurs, and kids need to be reminded of the basics. As one teenage boy said, "Reminding us when we first come in really helps." The key is to view the whole process as a zigzag progression of both human and leadership development.

Unique Program Variables

Problems are also associated with the almost infinite number of variables that crop up in different settings with different adult leaders, different kids, and different organizational structures and values. That's why "going to scale" with any framework is exceedingly difficult. If you were to visit our programs in Greensboro and Chicago, you might wonder how we can write a book that encompasses the purposes and processes of both sets of programs. Here are a few examples that emphasize the role of variables in our work:

- One of us works in a large very diverse city, the other in a midsized city. Both work with underserved kids, but the extent of support from schools and community agencies differs, as does the mobility of families.
- Both of us are employed at major universities, but only one of us has access to university facilities and transportation.
- Both of us work with graduate students in our programs, but one of us directs a very structured set of programs in which graduate students are assistant instructors who then help youth to transition to the self-actualized leadership stage. The other moves graduate students from being assistant instructors into directing their own programs as soon as possible, and encourages them to modify what they learned as an assistant instructor to make their new programs their own. One result of this approach is variability among the student-run programs, representing a range of personal preferences and judgments.

These specific examples illustrate the variables problems, but possible variables stretch far beyond these examples. The following categories cast a wider net of possible variables adult leaders may need to contend with.

Location: In general, the larger the city the more problems the adult leader needs to deal with, for example, gang issues, mobility of the kids, travel issues, suspicion of "outsiders" in the neighborhood, and difficulty of getting support from the often-beleaguered staff school and community-based organizations. All of these factors can affect youth leadership development.

One of us has directed programs in one of the largest cities in the country, but has also run programs in cities of about 70,000 as well as a town of 10,000. The smaller the city or town, the easier it was to get started offering a program. Doors opened almost directly in relation to city size. Organizations dedicated to serving or supporting underserved youth were very cooperative in meetings and joint projects, again proportional to city size.

Adult leader's professional role: Expectations as well as opportunities and limitations differ, depending on whether the adult leader is a coach, physical education teacher, youth worker, or university faculty member. For example, it is difficult to sidestep the issue of winning in organized sport as it is practiced in the United States. Having an empowerment-based leadership program reduces a coach's sense of being in charge, and therefore may not be very appealing to some coaches. Physical education teachers, on the other hand, must deal with large classes, school rules, and physical education standards and benchmarks. Youth leaders can really help if (a big if) the teacher can find a way to train them to lead and give them feedback (see chapter 11 on In-school Physical Education).

The kids: How old are the kids? Both genders? How about kids with ethnic-racial backgrounds that differ from the adult leader's background? Or kids from more than one ethnic-racial group? How many kids are in the group? As we have emphasized, group size dictates how relational a program leader can be. More than 15 or even fewer at one time and the program leader's ability to be relational is likely to be difficult. All of these factors as well as others can be potential problems for the adult leader to help youth leaders solve.

Adult assistance: The adult leader who is a "lone ranger has to be the 'whole show.' " All planning, implementation, evaluation, counseling, trouble-shooting (e.g., problem-solving), and public relations are his or her responsibilities, not to mention developing a leadership program. Assistants can help immensely with these responsibilities, for example, providing leadership for a smaller group as the youth leader struggles to take charge of the whole program. But finding competent, reliable assistants becomes one more job among many. It usually requires an in-depth interview and some training. Both of us have been "burned" by poor staff selection—a painful learning experience.

Administrative support: Administrative support can vary from strong support to benign neglect or even outright hostility to having this kind of leadership program. Walsh (2002) argued from his research that two kinds of administrative assistance are necessary to facilitate program success if the adult leader is not a staff member at the institution: The initial contact person who is the oversight administrator for such programs, and the secondary contact person who has direct contact with the kids. The adult leader who is already a staff member at a school or community, on the other hand, already has contacts and some sense of whatever issues or barriers might derail a youth leadership program and can plan based on these insights.

We have faced many problems with administrative support, as well as a few terrifically supportive administrators whom we cited in the Acknowledgments. Sometimes, with less supportive or even obstructionist administrators, we have been able to effectively implement a successful problem-solving process, other times not. For example, halfway through the year in an after-school program at an urban school, the vice principal pulled most of the kids out of one of our programs, explaining that the pressures of No Child Left Behind (NCLB) required that these kids work on their "numeracy" problems after school. NCLB also reduced another program to once a week, again because after-school time was needed to tutor the kids in test-related knowledge. This problem is partly about administrators not willing to "go to bat" for the program, but it also involves the overarching policies of the macro-organization discussed in the next section.

Administrative commitment and oversight are sometimes weak. In the following example, this problem sidelined one of our programs prematurely. A soccer club in an urban community-based organization led by a graduate student had to be abandoned when it became clear that, despite the agency director's glowing description of their youth development, the soccer club was the only program with any structure! A soccer leadership initiative had just begun, but as one of the novice leaders explained, no one wanted to have meetings and "learn things"; they just wanted to hang out with their friends like everyone else did.

In a nearby neighborhood, an after-school martial arts leadership club, treated with "benign neglect" by administrators and relegated to a classroom as its "gym," continued to operate over several years and gradually became a respected program in the school, receiving public recognition from the principal for promoting student leadership in her school.

There are no easy or generic answers here. The best we have been able to do is learn from these incidents, to persevere—to outlast the problems insofar as possible, and to close shop and move on to more promising sites when necessary. The only caution is to anticipate such problems, prepare for them (e.g., with solutions banks described next), and think carefully about possible alternatives.

Macro versus micro-programs: Micro- and macro-programs present different situations for problem-setting. A *micro-program* allows you to develop your own program however you want within some broad guidelines laid out by your host, whether it is a school, community agency, church gym, or other setting. Since you are a "visiting" program leader, guidelines are usually minimal. You are in charge of developing, implementing, and evaluating your curriculum; determining number of meetings per week as well as the length of each session and of the length of the program; and whatever work it takes to recruit kids, take care of permission slips, and whatever other rules your host requires. So you have a lot of freedom in most cases, but not much support. It is all up to you and anyone you can recruit to help you. Sympathetic administrators reduce your problems immensely.

Macro-programs, on the other hand, imply that you are a staff member of an organization with multiple programs that sometimes serve adults as well as kids. You have to fit in. Also, new programs sometimes threaten the status quo or the growth of an already established program. The institutional culture—as in "We've always done it this way"—and other duties deemed by administration to be more important than youth leadership can present obstacles. In macro-organizations with existing systems in place, especially in a less-than-supportive environment, the primary question is "What can I get away with?"—that is, what's possible in this setting? This sometimes leads to the development of programs that are perceived as "subversive activities" within the larger organization. Whether the introduction of a "different" program creates a conflict within the organization or not depends on many factors such as its compatibility with the macro-organization goals and processes, the extent of oversight, and the ever-present relational challenges associated with other staff as well as administrators.

One specific example of the differences between macro- and microprograms can be seen in a comparison of typical public schools with what were until recently referred to as alternative schools (Fantini, 1976; Raywid, 1994). Alternative schools historically presaged the youth development movement by implementing small classes in small schools and employing teachers who often taught different subjects and doubled (or tripled) as counselors, administrators, fund-raisers, and sometimes even lunch-servers. These schools offered a wide range of student-centered educational experiences characterized by empowering students to share their thoughts, make choices, and take on leadership positions; offering themed projects and classes; and using alternative assessment strategies to evaluate students' work such as individual culminating projects and written qualitative comments rather than grades on report cards. Sometimes these schools were sponsored by a school district, including schools-within-a-school; sometimes they were sponsored by not-for-profit organizations. In general, "they represented varying degrees of departure from standard school organization, programs, and environments" (Raywid, 1994, p. 26). Teacher certification varies from state to state, sometimes requiring adherence to state certification requirements, sometimes making school-by-school decisions based on faculty training and experiences. In one case, a noncertified teacher was approved based on her masters degree in education from Harvard; in another, approval was given to a teacher who had special training in working with kids who had emotional and social problems.

Recently, different kinds of public and private small schools have proliferated to meet the needs of kids who require more attention and guidance than a public school system can provide—including charter schools, contract schools, and performance schools. These small schools can be further divided by the *kind* of charter, contract, or performance standards being used. They also vary in curriculum requirements, funding, teacher and principal certification requirements, teacher union involvement, governance, and accountability. This recent small school trend is not without controversy, as reflected in responses to the small school movement from both the right and the left (Ayers & Klonsky, 2006; Duncan, 2006; Klonsky & Klonsky, 2008).

Unlike typical public schools, physical education may not be offered, may be substituted for by a recreation time, or may be taught by teachers certified in other subjects. One of us taught part-time in alternative schools for ten years with an expired Ohio physical education certificate and an advanced degree in physical education but no current state certification. No one ever raised this question! He also got roped into teaching history and team teaching sex education! (See Don's alternative school physical education story in chapter 11.)

Youth Leader Issues

How can an adult leader provide the day-to-day guidance necessary for the kind of leadership we have in mind? Empowerment, for example, requires a degree of risk. In a public high school program, one of us caused the teacher who agreed to co-teach a leadership class to walk out of the gym halfway through the lesson. Afterward, she simply said "I couldn't handle all that freedom!" If a skeptical administrator had observed this scene, the program could have been shut down.

Although TPSR and the leadership stages leave room for adjustments and new ideas, they don't always give sufficient guidance in confronting any number of issues that arise when kids attempt to take on leadership. In a perfect world, each issue would go through a careful problem-setting process before asking kids to lead. In the very imperfect process-oriented world of youth work and with developing young leaders in particular, we often have to try to help the youth leader solve the problem immediately without taking charge ourselves. For example, if a fight breaks out, on-the-spot action is necessary, if not by the youth leader then by the adult leader. One's lesson or program plan won't ordinarily provide much guidance here. This kind of spontaneous, immediate response is best described by Schon (1987), when he compared reflection-in-action to knowing-in-action (Schon, 1987, p. 26; as cited in Hellison, 2003, p. 83): "[Knowing-in-action means we] have learned how to do something, we can execute smooth sequences of activity, recognition, decision, and adjustment without having, as we say, to 'think about it'... [Reflection-in-action, on the other hand, refers to a period of time] during which we can still make a difference to the situation at hand—our thinking serves to reshape what we are doing while we are doing it."

Reflection-in-action is called for when there is no time to problem-set. It involves recognizing a problem and immediately conducting an on-the-spot experiment, leaving the in-depth reflective process for later. Adult leaders need to become skilled in reflection-in-action so that youth leaders can learn from them. However, prevention is better than remediation whenever possible. One way to alert youth leaders to anticipate problems that might arise is to help them create a solutions bank (adapted from Orlick, 1980). A solutions bank starts with a list of problematic incidents that a youth leader might face in the upcoming program. This list might include help with solving conflicts and arguments without taking over, sustaining the leadership role in spite of attractive options (e.g., being a participant versus a leader), or facing intimidation perceived or real from older or more skilled kids. After this list is generated, possible solutions for each problem are explored. The point is not that the solutions will work, but that this process can mentally and emotionally prepare the adult leader for such issues, whether the specific solution on the list is used or not. It is, in a sense, warming up for the next inning, helping the youth worker be more confident in his or her plan for the day and ability to deal with problems. A shortcut to creating a solutions bank is to ask the youth leader "If [such-and-such] happens, what will you do?"

When reflection-in-action goes awry, pre-post program reflection can help. Pre- and post-program reflection builds reflection time into the process in two ways. Pre-program reflection helps the youth leader get mentally prepared for the next session by processing recent difficulties in the program and then thinking ahead, which could lead to creation of a solutions bank. Post-program reflection is an opportunity for the youth leader to assess what went on in that session while it is still fresh. The key question to the youth leader is: Is what you're doing working? Or: To what extent did the plan for today work? Why or why not? What issues needed attention, how were they handled, do we need to revisit them in our next session? What should our plan for the next session entail?

We believe that all kids can lead, but they will likely be at different developmental stages. One strategy that addresses this individualized process is to prepare individual very brief "lesson plans" for each youth leader and potential youth leader in the program. For example, perhaps one participant has shown absolutely no interest in or talent for leading others. With some urging and assistance, he may be willing to take on a small leadership role in the awareness talk by telling everyone one thing that everyone should focus on that day, especially if he is coached ahead of time. A quick debriefing meeting afterward can help these tentative kids to reflect on their reluctance, how it felt to lead, and what the next steps might be. For leaders who begin to show some arrogance as a leader, a very different plan is needed, perhaps requiring a confrontational wakeup call regarding their leadership responsibilities.

Reflective insights, knowledge of past experiences, and imagination/creativity all help in solving problems. Adult leaders often have to take the initiative, but knowing when to give way to youth leaders is crucial to their development. Ruffini (1980, p. 103) pointed out some of the needed adult leadership skills: "At times we must listen facilitatively...[Sometimes we must]...confront students without injuring the student-teacher relationship...or the self-esteem of the student."

At times the experiential trial and error approach, which is admittedly risky for many, produces a better way of doing things. The most vivid example for one of your authors is summarized by an excerpt describing his early experiences with underserved youth: "I had taught in two other [underserved] youth programs...[and] therefore had some notion of what to expect (or so I thought) and what to do...The only problem [in my current program] was that nothing seemed to work...I was forced back to the drawing board day after day, tightening here, inserting something new there, until I had worn a deep groove between [ideas] and practice" (Hellison, 1978, p. vi). Out of that often-painful year-long experience, TPSR was born, and it has provided guidance for all of his youth programs since that time some thirty years ago. Perhaps a better approach to youth leadership could emerge in the same way.

Insights and Take-aways

While frameworks like TPSR and the Leadership stages provide guidance, problems inevitably arise. We believe that whenever possible, the adult leader as well as youth leaders should problem-set before attempting to problem-solve.

- Youth leadership problems can be loosely categorized as building a TPSR foundation for the leadership program, addressing program variables, and dealing with day-to-day youth leadership issues while teaching youth leaders how to solve problems that occur as part of their leadership responsibilities.
- Building a TPSR foundation can be based on a TPSR sport club as we have done or can start with a leadership club that progressively involves both TPSR principles and the leadership stages.

- Addressing program variables forces adult leaders to attend to their locations, professional roles, kids in the program, adult assistance or going it alone, administrative supports, and whether they have to contend with macro- or micro-programs.
- Helping youth leaders to solve problems involves, among other things, modeling successful strategies for potential youth leaders, teaching young leaders how to create solutions banks, experience in pre- and post-reflection, utilizing the different strategies needed to address individual progress and issues, and confronting contentious attitudes in an appropriate way.

11
In-school Physical Education

Teaching is hard. Some days you'll have good days and some days you'll have bad days.

—Youth Leader Corps member

In-school physical education has one clear advantage over after-school and summer programs: It reaches most students who attend public schools. As sport psychologists Shields and Bredemeier (1995) argued, "Physical education remains the largest organized setting for physical activity" (p. 199).

In-school Physical Education Issues

A number of caveats need to be appended to the above statement. The physical education requirement has eroded over the past several years, so that fewer days and hours per year are required in many states. Younger kids, who arguably would benefit significantly from having a strong program that encourages rather than discourages active participation, often get less time and instruction than older students who, as one eighth grader commented, "are pretty set in our ways!" Other problems exist as well. Class size, while occasionally smaller, often consists of thirty or more students, putting a strain on the development of teacher-student relationships. Elementary physical education teachers have one advantage: They usually teach the same students for several years, which provides a more relational environment over time. In addition to school-wide rules (which are numerous in most schools), physical education has its own set of rules, some which pertain to safety, some to management (and control). Taken together, teachers are faced with a long list of "don'ts" to enforce. The dreary and sometimes abusive stories told by some, perhaps many, adults about their years as physical education students certainly don't help either.

Countless rules are one problem, dysfunctional practices another; "Rolling out the ball" (translation: substitute play for learning) has been a pervasive criticism of physical education programs, as has the negative attitude engendered in many students by all the traditional trappings of a physical education class—uniforms, showers (if available), squads, whistles, long lines, and competitive tournaments favored by the more athletic (and most vocal) students.

In-school physical education must also deal with some of the variables described in the Problem-solving chapter, such as:

- The ideal versus real professional role of the teacher who is sometimes viewed as manager of recreation breaks.
- The school as macro-program with many programs under one roof (e.g., classes, special education and gifted programs, in-school suspension rooms, interscholastic athletic teams, intramural teams, clubs).
- Oversight by a central administration.
- Competition for space and recognition.

As the problem-solving chapter points out, physical education teachers must deal with physical education standards and benchmarks imposed by the state, district, or national professional organization such as the National Association of Sport and Physical Education.

Youth Leadership in In-School Physical Education

Youth leaders could really help teachers deal with class size, provide some individualized attention and instruction, and curb some discipline problems. However, organizing a youth leader program as a teacher is no easy task in an in-school setting. First of all, it is one more thing to do, and it can get complicated. Students need to be trained to be leaders and be given feedback on their performance. If the teacher wants to introduce cross-age teaching, organizational issues mount, including finding time to select and train physical education leaders, locating a teacher of younger kids who is willing to collaborate, and finding the time and space to run the program. Despite the difficulties, the following ideas and examples suggest that youth leadership can become part of an in-school program.

The Influence of School Size and Purpose on Youth Leadership

One of us (Don) began as a physical education teacher in three high-need high schools, where a rudimentary form of TPSR initially evolved. Faced with the difficulty of reaching these young people and in particular not being able to give them some life skills to assist in navigating the violence, peer pressure, weak teaching, and other forces in the community, these early years were filled with experimentation, setbacks, and a great deal of learning what works and, often painfully, what doesn't. The earliest version of TPSR (Hellison, 1978) did not specify leadership as a student goal. It wasn't until the early '80s in an alternative school physical education program (Hellison, 1985a) that leadership became a part of responsibility level four, complementing the related level four values of "caring" and "concern for others." His experience in the small alternative school was so powerful that he stayed there for eight years, ran an after-school martial arts program, and occasionally taught history and sex ed as well as physical education. Following that experience he spent two more years at other alternative schools (Hellison, 1988).

Both of these settings, urban and alternative high schools, served similar low income and often alienated students, but these two settings differed substantially in class size. The typical high school physical education class was thirty to forty, whereas the alternative school limited class size to a maximum of fifteen and offered more flexibility in planning and offering PE classes. Class size influences the extent and quality of relational time with individual students and especially the guidance of students through the leadership development stages. In contrast to alternative schools, mainstream public schools also tend to have a "deep culture" regarding what and how to teach and an informal socialization process that "inducts" new teachers into a system that at least in some schools discourages innovation.

In essence, the teacher can do more with less in alternative settings, whereas class size, the school culture, and specific curriculum guidelines in public schools tend to reduce TPSR to "TPSR Lite." Nevertheless, in-school physical education is by far the best way to reach almost all kids, even if the experience is not in depth. As Shields and Bredemeier argued (1995, p. 199), "[in-school] physical education is probably the most significant physical activity context for developing moral character."

While the alternative school offered an excellent opportunity to develop youth leadership, the how-to was missing for the most part.

In both settings, Don's early leadership strategy was expressed well by one student who said, "You just threw us in there!" Yet even with its imperfections, "throwing them in there" without much structure offered more responsibility-based leadership than student athletes leading prescribed calisthenics, which was the usual practice in public schools at that time.

Fortunately, a few more structured strategies were attempted as years passed, slightly fattening a malnourished "bag of tricks" for promoting youth leadership in school programs. Nascent forms of leadership were developing "on the fly," presaging more developed forms such as reciprocal coaching, peer coaching, peer teaching, and cross-age teaching.

Most of these leadership experiences provided a bit more focus and guidance than "just throwing them in there," and with a heavy dose of self-reflection, students and the teacher were able to pick up the pieces afterward and take a baby step forward. During this process of learning how to teach leadership, some more sophisticated strategies were gradually attempted. For example, a lightweight version of pre-student teaching was offered on a voluntary basis in the alternative high school followed by an after-school cross-age teaching experience with fourth graders. Pre-student teaching consisted of planning a lesson and teaching it to peers while being videotaped. Eight students chose to participate, all of whom completed the pre-student teaching experience. Seven of the eight traveled to a nearby elementary school to teach, while one, who did not feel ready to teach, volunteered to drive. This experience was repeated several times in different programs, but never with more than one teaching experience per year due to the difficulty of organizing the cross-age teaching experiences. By contrasting this with the much more robust leadership stages described in earlier chapters, it is evident that our approach to leadership has come a long way.

A final point here is that alternative schools provide the flexibility needed to experiment or explore new ideas for educating our young people. One of these ideas is to have youth leadership development as an integral part of a school's curriculum. Within the past decade we have seen increased support for alternative schools (e.g., The Bill and Melinda Gates Foundation), especially for those schools that address drop-out prevention. This support has given great promise for creating new school initiatives like charter schools, as well as well as early and middle colleges. For example, Tom is presently creating an alternative high school (middle college) for at-risk youth on his university campus. By being located on a university campus, the school will not only provide students with a taste of college life, but serve as a clinical site for professional teaching programs. Although state guidelines for academic curriculum development must be followed, the pathways for doing this can be varied to suit the needs of the students. Youth leadership development will be an integral part of the school's overall mission. The four stages of leadership development will guide the planning and implementation of leadership experiences during in-school physical education, after-school sport clubs, and community internship programs.

In-school TPSR Programs

TPSR has also been adopted and adapted by in-school physical education teachers across the United States and in several other countries. While by no means a dominant teaching approach, comments from teachers strongly suggest that it has a presence in many states and a number of other countries. Since systematic research has not been conducted, there is no telling what really goes on in many of these programs. Ideally, adoption of TPSR ought to indicate at least a modest student leadership component, since helping others and leadership is one of the five levels of responsibility in the TPSR model. The reality may be quite different, or more likely mixed, depending on the program.

A study by Mrugala (2002) shed some light on the state of TPSR implementation in the United States. Since no complete list of physical education teachers using TPSR was available, Mrugala based his study on a purposive sample of physical education teachers who claim to use TPSR. He sent a qualitative in-depth internet survey to sixty teachers, 52 of whom completed the survey. Most of the respondents were elementary school physical education teachers. His findings were numerous but in most cases beyond our focus here. However, some are relevant. Almost all the respondents initially adopted TPSR to improve their discipline strategies, but 60% reported "placing more emphasis *on teaching helping* [italics ours], caring, respect, responsibility, and cooperation" (p. 100). Some noticed themselves becoming more relational with the kids and viewing them more holistically, rather than as "phys ed" students. Youth leadership comments were largely limited to the italicized words above, but one wrote that "students have a much bigger role in keeping the class running smoothly" (p. 101). Since most were elementary students, it's not surprising that leadership was not a primary goal (although we have had some success with kids as young as ten years old taking on some limited leadership roles).

Other in-school physical education teachers have also ventured into teaching leadership. Middle school physical education Teacher of the Year John Hichwa's book, *Right Fielders Are People Too* (1998), offered what he called "an inclusive approach to teaching middle school physical education," stating up front that he teaches children *first*, not motor skills and fitness. The core of teaching children for John is his version of the three Rs: Teaching kids to be respectful, responsible, and resourceful. John contrasted his three Rs in physical education with a very different definition: Take Role, Roll out the ball, and Read the newspaper! His emphasis on teaching children first, as well as his detailed description of the three Rs, suggest similarities to several elements of TPSR, and his debriefing sessions parallel TPSR's reflection time. He stressed and based grades in part on being "thoughtful and helpful to others" (p. 45), which is a first step in leadership development. However, his most important innovation for leadership development was to divide the class into three groups, two of which depend on student leadership while the third group works with John, thereby personalizing instruction and increasing relational time. When groups rotate throughout the week, John has the opportunity to personalize instruction for each group. From our perspective, his three-group strategy creates a unique opportunity for developing leadership in in-school physical education.

Daryl Siedentop's sport education (Siedentop, 1998), which has been one of the most popular curriculum models in physical education, took leadership further than Hichwa, although sport education's purpose—to socialize students in the best of the organized sport culture—differs widely from the purpose of both TPSR and Hichwa's *Right fielders are people too*. In sport education, units become sport seasons with teams practicing, playing preseason games, in-season games, and an end-of-season tournament. Typically, students are coaches of three teams formed from the class roster, and they also referee, keep team statistics, and assume responsibility for other tasks necessary to conduct an organized sport program.

In-school Youth Leadership Programs in Other Countries

Murray Turner, a New Zealand high school physical education teacher, took a three-day TPSR workshop, and subsequently, as a national moderator of the leadership assessment for New Zealand's national qualifications, authored a masters thesis, "Investigating student leadership in senior high school physical education" (Turner, 2007). His thesis focused on the relationship between social responsibility and leadership among student leaders in physical education. The leadership requirement is based on a specific New Zealand educational learning standard, "Demonstrate leadership in physical activity," which included this progression:

- Introduce leadership roles.
- Participate in a practical demonstration of leadership that becomes more complex across three levels and includes (1) understanding how individuals in groups influence relationships, beliefs, and self worth; and (2) coaching teams and applying interpersonal skills in managing others.
- Critically and reflectively examine effective relationships in physical education leadership.

Murray's investigation resulted in recommendations for more emphasis on evaluating leadership in practical situations rather than using academic exercises, and arguing that leadership is best learned by applying and constructing knowledge in practice. He pointed out that focusing on the whole person was the most effective educational youth leadership approach and that self-efficacy was a major predictor of leadership success.

Bailey (2008) traced the role of sport and physical education's contribution to the conceptual and empirical development of social inclusion as social policy in the United Kingdom. While not focusing directly on the role of youth leadership, Siedentop's sport education, Ennis's Sport for Peace (Ennis et al., 1999), and Hellison's TPSR were used to develop school-based physical education initiatives, suggesting that youth leadership, a prominent aspect of all three models, was at the very least part of the conversation leading to research and development activities.

A related concern in the UK, disaffected youth, resulted in Living for Sport, an initiative of the Youth Sport Trust that involved over 300 schools (Sandford, Armour, & Duncombe, 2008). Eleven- to 16-year-olds were targeted for behavior improvement in these schools. Sport activities involved goal-setting and involved working toward organizing a culminating event.

> Findings...provide some support for the notion that physical activity programs can facilitate positive personal and social development in

young people, particularly in terms of improving confidence, developing communication, teamwork, and *leadership skills* [italics ours], and encouraging behavioral improvement (Sandford, Armour, & Duncombe, 2008, p. 106).

Mandigo and his associates (Mandigo, Corlett, & Anderson, 2008) reported the development of Quality Physical Education (QPE), a program model based on promoting peace education internationally through physical activity. Leadership was one of several life skills that were embedded in physical activity programs designed to promote peace education. The authors collaborated with the Ministry of Education in war-torn El Salvador to promote peace-building. The youth leadership component consisted of support and resources for youth leaders working for several El Salvador ministries in both urban and rural areas. These youth leaders were able to work with local gangs who controlled many of these areas. Systematic evaluation of this initiative is limited but promising, given the situation in El Salvador and the need for peace.

Insights and Take-aways

In-school physical education offers the best opportunity to reach all kids, although a number of potential barriers reduce the likelihood of developing youth leadership programs. A youth leadership program, if able to surmount the highly structured and rule-bound circumstances of many schools could be very helpful as assistant teachers, allowing the teacher to focus on less engaged students and to develop stronger relationships with all kids in class.

Based on the experiences of one of us, alternative schools provided what he still believes is the best way to reach kids, because it offers more structure than after-school programs (e.g., ready access to kids in a holistic setting) but at the same time smaller class sizes and, depending on the state, fewer restrictions (e.g., rules and traditions) compared to typical public schools. Being able to explore the potential of youth leadership in an alternative school opened the door to more developed forms of youth leadership in subsequent years.

Alternative schools are not typical public schools. Can public school physical education teach youth leadership? A study of TPSR implementation in in-school physical education provided some evidence for lead-up youth leadership activities, but programs only tangentially related to TPSR have been implemented to varying degrees in in-school physical education. Sport education and Sport for Peace are good examples of providing leadership opportunities for kids in physical education. Turner's very structured approach in New Zealand physical education addressed youth leadership in great detail, although direct leadership experience was limited in its initial implementation. Other initiatives such as the instructional strategies in *Right fielders are people too*, and the in-school physical initiatives in the United Kingdom and El Salvador also have shown promise, and even a suggestion of nascent leadership. Taken together, in-school physical education can be a setting conducive to youth leadership depending on the context and of course the teacher.

IV

Is It Working?

12
Assessment

Nobody grew taller from being measured.

—Phillip Gammage

We are often asked "How do you know that your leadership programs are making a difference?" Or, we will hear the query "what kind of instruments, tests, and measures do you have to assess leadership development." These are fair questions and certainly remind us that others like professors, practitioners, parents, agency staff, and perhaps, youth leaders, want to see tangible results. More than likely, these results are expected to come from various paper-and-pencil or online measures. However, we have found that assessment of certain aspects of our leadership programs can be messy business and does not always lead to "tangible" outcomes. Getting things right takes time—sometimes years! Immediate results sometimes fade after a few weeks. Or the opposite occurs: results don't become apparent for months or even years.

We also realize that assessment is an essential part of leadership development. Probably one of the most important reasons we assess our youth leadership programs is to improve our work with young people. The stages described in the previous chapters undergo continuous change because we see that some ideas are not working or that certain goals are not being met. Very often assessment occurs on the spot because something needs to be fixed right away. When things are not working because of poor matching (e.g., in peer teaching), unclear directions by the adult leader, peer coaches who are too competitive, or inappropriate learning tasks by the leaders, immediate attention is required. This is called formative assessment. Other changes are linked to long-term observation, where patterns (some good, some not so good) begin to emerge. This type of assessment tends to be more formal and systematic and is generally referred to as summative assessment. In general, we believe that the products that come from any form of assessment can (and should) be used for some or all of the following reasons:

- assess needs,
- document how well your program is going,
- determine usefulness of a particular strategy,
- examine how certain parts of the leadership program (e.g., cross-age leading, community service, internship) are working, or
- provide information for modifying program goals (Hellison et al., 2000).

Assessment is no stranger to our youth leaders (and other students). Indeed, testing has become the prime "modis operandi" in today's school systems. In addition, the "Know Child Left Behind" (NCLB) federal mandate has added new weight to the influx of testing done in our school systems. The schools that our leaders attend (when they attend) sometimes assess their students, teachers, and content of class instruction. Other school districts administer state standards tests as well as the federally mandated NCLB, putting pressure on low performing schools to raise scores or risk being reconstituted or closed. Much of the focus of school-based assessment these days is on student performance (Hellison, 2003).

For youth leadership development programs to be effective, assessment must extend beyond test scores. Three elements have to be assessed: (1) youth leaders, (2) adult leader, and (3) overall program. Because of our values-based approach to youth leadership development, all of these areas need to be evaluated in different ways. The late Michael Scriven once pointed out that rather than being faithful to just one model of assessment, you must be faithful to the characteristics of your program (Scriven, 1997). If Scriven is right (and we think he is), then a "real world" view needs to be adopted so multiple choices and decisions in the assessment process can be recognized and dealt with. This allows those who work with kids to attend to multiple roles, values, and situations inherent in youth leadership programming. Thus, both traditional and non traditional or "creative" methods must come into play (Patton, 1989). This chapter provides an array of ideas that we and others have used to tap into what is happening, how attitudes and values are being affected, and to what extent relationships are thriving.

Assessment of the Youth Leader

Youth leader assessment should be consistent with the values of both TPSR and the stages of youth leadership development. To insure this, two things need to be present when evaluating your leaders. First, feedback on their development as responsible leaders needs to be given by you, the adult leader. Your feedback needs to be honest but also to include supportive messages of confidence and assurance. Second, ample opportunity for the leaders to be part of the evaluation process should be provided. For program participants to gain a foothold in their development as leaders, self evaluation through group meeting discussion and personal reflection is extremely important. Additionally, your direct feedback becomes an essential information source for the leader. These two sources of feedback provide important balance to the overall assessment of your leaders.

Group Meeting and Reflection Time

In the early chapters we talked about the importance of having a group meeting and reflection time after each developmental stage experience. Recall that group meetings allow the leaders to evaluate how their session went and discuss specific issues that emerged during the session.

There are usually two phases to the group meeting. During the first phase, all leaders have the opportunity to tell how their mini-lesson, team coaching, or cross-age lesson went—their self-assessment. They should also be encouraged to share ways in which individuals made positive contributions to the lesson and game. During the next phase, you (adult leader) should offer feedback. This should always come last since you are the only adult voice in the process. Starting the meeting with your feedback will only diffuse the leaders' willingness to share his or her thoughts, thus short circuiting the entire process.

During cross-age leading, another form of group feedback is to have the young children talk about how their leaders did. You can do this a couple of ways. One simple way is to have the children be part of the group meeting. Here, they can share their thoughts about the leaders. You can ask them questions about their leader's teaching

YOUTH LEADER THOUGHTS

Please answer the following questions:

1. How well did your lesson go today?

Why do you feel this way? Give examples.

2. What things do your need to work on?

3. What activities did you teach today? What goal(s) did each activity include?

4. How did your camp talk go today?

Give examples of what went well or didn't go well.

5. Give any examples how you really helped someone out today.

Figure 12.1 Youth leader self-assessment rating form

like, "What kinds of things did you learn from your leader today?" or "In what ways did your leader make your experience a positive one today?" or "What were some of the goals that your leader had you work on today?"

Another form of group feedback is to have it take place in a smaller group. You can have the leaders meet with their "home group" prior to a large group meeting. Small groups meetings sometimes lend themselves to greater response from the younger children.

A more effective way to do leader assessment is through self-reflection. Self-reflection requires the leaders to evaluate themselves

NAME: _____
DATE: _____

1. Were you on time today?

    Yes _____   No _____

2. What percent of the time did you provide leadership for the kids?

    All the time _____   Most of the time _____
    Some of the time _____   None of the time _____

3. What percent of the time were the kids at your station active (doing something related to basketball)?

    Almost all the time _____   Most of the time _____
    Less than half of the time _____

4. How positive were you with the kids?

    A lot _____   Some _____   Not much _____

5. How many kids' names do you know? _____

Figure 12.2   Apprentice teacher self-evaluation form

on how well they lead the younger children and, to some extent, how they imparted TPSR values to them. In chapter 7 we described different ways reflection can be facilitated during cross-age leadership. Journaling, self-ratings (e.g., four Bs in leader notebooks), and nonverbal responses to adult-leader questions (thumbs up, thumbs down, thumbs sideways) all work well here. Figures 12.1 and 12.2 show a combination of assessment formats that was used in Chicago's Apprentice Teachers (Cutforth & Puckett, 1999) and Greensboro's Youth Leader Corps programs.

Adult-Leader's Assessment of the Youth Leader

We (and our assistants) have also used various methods to evaluate our leaders. When we evaluate our leaders we do it with the intention of monitoring their progress. However, some personalizing is fine here. What we mean is that some leaders will quickly withdraw if they think that they are continually getting some kind of rating or grade from you. So critical feedback needs to be tempered by conveying confidence they are capable of leading. Obviously, this is extremely important if leaders are to progress through the various stages of development. The important issue here is that you do not want them to form the impression that you are evaluating them against some standard for everything they do. They get plenty of that in their schools.

There will be various "lenses" through which you can view the leaders' progress. One simple approach is to rate each individual leader's overall performance after each program session (leave a little room

Date_____ Assistant_____

Youth Leader_____ Lesson_____

Circle one.   Rate the quality of leadership on the following:

		Not Very Well		Moderately Well		Excellent
1.	Instructing Activities	1	2	3	4	5
2.	Leading Reflection	1	2	3	4	5
3.	Communicating effectively with	1	2	3	4	5
4.	Reinforcing the values of the club (modeling, stating goals)	1	2	3	4	5

Please:

1. State the strengths of the lesson (in terms of teacher behavior and student learning).

2. State two things that the teacher can improve on (in terms of teacher behavior and student learning).

3. Describe how well the participants responded to the teacher during the lesson and camp talk.

4. Is there anything that happened today that affected the quality of the experiences?

5. What do you think the youth leader gained from the experience today?

Figure 12.3 Adult leader's assessment of leadership development

for comments)—for example 5=great; 4=some great stuff was evident; 3=lesson went well as expected; 2=some struggles were evident; 1= not a good day). A sheet of paper on your clipboard with each of the leader's names will nicely work here. As another example, in Chicago a martial arts leadership workbook contains a list of skills to be learned in order to become a competent martial artist, for example, the fighting stance. Leaders rate themselves on a continuum of: (1) Haven't practiced, (2) Working on it, (3) Can demonstrate it, (4) Can apply it in a controlled situation, and (5) Can teach it. A more formal assessment that can be used by adult leaders is given in figure 12.3. This instrument provides both ratings and qualitative assessment data.

Name of student_____

Teacher_____

Administration time: 1st____ 2nd____ 3rd____ 4th____

Indicate (by circling a number) how hard the club member above tried during the past nine weeks on the following items:

	Never				Often
Paid attention	1	2	3	4	5
Began work immediately	1	2	3	4	5
Followed directions	1	2	3	4	5
Was sensitive to other's feelings	1	2	3	4	5
Helped classmates	1	2	3	4	5
Turned in assignments	1	2	3	4	5
Persisted rather than gave up when tasks got difficult	1	2	3	4	5
Worked independently	1	2	3	4	5
Was not easily discouraged	1	2	3	4	5

Number of office referrals _____

Comments:

Figure 12.4   Trying in the classroom inventory

Another approach to assessing leadership performance is to look at how the leadership experiences are impacting the leaders' work at school. This approach has been especially useful for assessing kids who are involved in stage one experiences—Learning to take responsibility. Using the "Trying in the Classroom Inventory" (TCI) (Project Effort, 2000) classroom teachers are asked to rate the club members' classroom performance at the end of each grading period (see figure 12.4). The TCI taps into the student's ability to gain control over various aspects of social and academic classroom outcomes. With slight modification, the TCI could also be used by the physical education teacher as well.

On occasion we have used focus and individual interviews to assess the leaders' growth in leadership. This approach allowed us to delve a little deeper into some of the psycho-social factors (e.g., relationships, program environment and organization, personalities) that reflect and influence a leader's commitment to the leadership program (Schilling, 2001; Schilling, Martinek, & Carson, 2007). For example, Tammy Schilling, in her assessment of the leaders' commitment to the Greensboro's leadership program, developed a set of questions that guided individual and focus group interviews. The questions posed to the leaders were open-ended like:

- What are the reasons for being committed or not committed to the program?
- What are the factors that influence your commitment to the program?
- How would you compare leaders who are more committed to the program to those that are the least committed?

There are a number ways in which interview data can be organized so that meaning from the leaders' responses can be discerned (see Schilling, 2001; Martinek, Schilling, & Hellison, 2006). You can choose to use informal ways to organize data such as simply placing the individual responses into larger categories (e.g., relationships, personal characteristics). Or you can use more systematic procedures that follow stricter guidelines for data analysis (see Lincoln & Guba, 1985; Gould, Finch, & Jackson, 1993). The method you select will depend on how you plan to use the data and the audience with whom you will be sharing the data. A good rule of thumb is: if the data is for your staff and other adult leaders—keep it simple. If you are trying to place assessment results in a grant proposal or research journal—use a more formal approach.

A Word about School Performance Measures

We are frequently asked if our leadership programs have an impact on the leaders' school performance, especially grades and test scores. In response to this question, we first tell people that it would be nice if all our leaders were potential honor roll students. But the truth is, many of the kids with whom we work struggle academically for a number of reasons, not the least of which is their (and our) mistrust in the school's evaluation process.

Alfie Kohn (1999) does a great job of showing how grades have been scientifically proven to reduce students' interest in learning, preferences for challenging tasks, and quality of thinking. And yet, schools (and funding agencies) still place great emphasis on the importance and validity of grading. Therefore, low grades tend not to vary among the leaders from year to year. But more importantly for us, grades and test scores don't tell us a lot about their abilities to apply the values of responsible, caring, and compassionate leadership in their schools. That is, they don't tell us about their willingness (and courage) to discourage their peers from joining a gang. And, they fail to tell us the level of responsibility it takes for a leader to get his or her siblings ready for school, escort them to the bus stop every morning, and then get themselves to school on time. And, they fail to tap into the level of compassion it takes to help a classmate deal with his or her personal problems. The best indicators have been those impromptu testimonies, small notes, and phone calls from principals, counselors, teachers, parents, and peers who share those actions that illustrate the positive impact your leaders are capable of having on others.

Assessment of the Adult-leader

Both of us are fully aware that assessment of the adult leader is as necessary as it is for youth leaders. A first step in this process is to self-assess your own personal values. In chapter 1 we described three beliefs about kids that adult leaders need to have if they are to be successful program leaders (i.e., kids are capable of leading, caring for others, & making good decisions). Knowing that these values are squarely in place during program planning is a good start in the self-assessment process.

You will also find that there are other ways of assessing your effectiveness as an adult leader. For example, you can continually examine how you are doing by giving yourself a grade after every session (did we say we are against giving grades?!). This allows you to become more informed about things that need work. You could grade on how well you handled a particular situation (e.g., a leader who develops a negative attitude) or how well you were able to orchestrate the group meeting. The problem that both of us have had in doing this, however, is that we tend to give ourselves low grades throughout the semester. You may find that you, too, will be your own worst critic. It is a good idea, therefore, to revisit the last chapter on adult-leader youth-leader relationship skills. This will help guide your responses to self evaluations.

Another way to self assess is by quizzing yourself using the questions in table 12.1. The questions were originally developed by Don (Hellison, 2003) to evaluate leadership qualities for those teaching in TPSR sport programs. The questionnaire has been somewhat modified to fit the context of a youth leadership program.

If all your responses to the questions can be either "yes" or "I am working on it" or "I want to do a better job on that" then you are on the right track! Don has further expanded the response set to assess your "specific readiness" by checking off one of the following categories for each statement:

- I am doing this now,
- I want to do this soon,
- This a long-range goal for me,
- I am not sure, let me think about it, or
- This doesn't apply to my program (Hellison, 2003, p. 119).

Assessment of the Program

All of the ideas for assessment that we have described provided thus far can (and should) be a part of what you do in your program. That is, reflection, journaling, note taking, and group discussion are integral parts of the overall operation of your leadership program! At some point, however, you will be asked to provide an overall assessment of your program. Funding agencies will no doubt require some kind of detailed assessment that tells them whether certain goals were met.

Formal program assessment can be a challenging task, especially if you are immersed in day-to-day operations. In some cases, it may be better to have someone from the outside evaluate the program although there are shortcomings in using this approach. One is that outsiders are not intimately connected with your program. This

Table 12.1 Adult-leader questionnaire

1. Do you like kids and can relate to them?
2. Do you try to treat all your leaders "unequally but fairly" (that is to say, individually)?
3. Do you spend some time focusing on the leaders' strengths?
4. Do you listen to your leaders—believe that they know things?
5. Do you share power with your leaders?
6. Are the leaders learning to include all their kids in the activities?
7. Are the leaders learning to control their negative statements and temper, rather than relying on you to take control?
8. Do your leaders have an opportunity to work on their own goals?
9. Do your leaders have a voice in evaluating the program and solving problems that arise?
10. Do the leaders have ample opportunity to teach and lead?
11. Do you try to emphasize the idea to your leaders of transfer from program to life?
12. Do your leaders leave your program understanding the responsibility of being a leader?

makes it difficult for them to effectively translate their findings to the specific nuances of the program.

Many of our colleagues in the sciences would argue that having an outside person removes any bias during the evaluation process. We argue, however, that there is nothing wrong with having bias. In fact, there is no such thing as being unbiased in youth work. You can, however, get multiple perspectives if others observe your program which may suggest some things you have overlooked or some blind spots in your self-assessment. Still, it is important to identify things that you struggle with in your program. After all, you are the one most familiar with the information already collected including anecdotal records from group and individual discussions. Both of us believe that if you truly want the outcomes of your assessment efforts to impact the quality of your program, you must become involved with the development and delivery of the program assessment plan and application of its outcomes.

A good starting point is to find out whether your program is doing what you want it do. If your program is doing something different from what you intended, then your leadership program will probably not work! It is not unusual to find program directors rush in with an armful of measuring tools only to find little effect from the program. The leadership program that we are talking about here may not have, in fact, been implemented at all. For example, in Buchanan's dissertation (1996), she trained adult leaders to implement TPSR and then assessed the impact of their programs. The impact of TPSR on kids was minimal, but she learned that the trainers had difficulty giving up their control and therefore did not implement TPSR except in bits and pieces. That's why it is important to separate the fidelity of your program from its impact (Hellison, 2003).

Program Outcome Model

Once you have determined the extent to which your leadership program is being implemented, you can follow some other procedures that provide a more detailed picture of what your program is accomplishing. One model that has been used to guide program evaluation is the Program Outcome Model (United Way of Greater Greensboro, 2001). In fact, many granting agencies (local and federal) often require that this model be included in grant requests. The figure below (figure 12.5) provides a flow chart of various parts of the model that can be included in the assessment process.

The "Input" part of the Greensboro model pertains to the resources that are needed to run the program (e.g., money, staff and staff time, volunteers, space). Constraints are also considered here. For example, one of the constraints that we have encountered with our summer

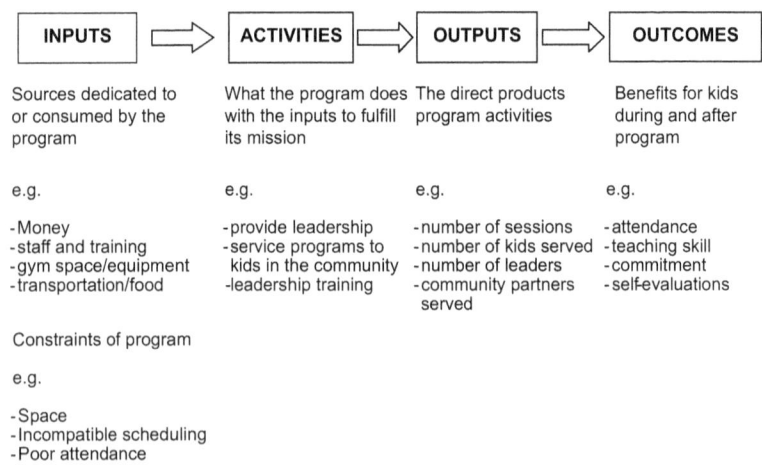

Figure 12.5   Program outcome model

leadership programs was working around the scheduling of space for other programs operating at our universities (NYSP, athletic sport camps, classes). Another constraint was the lack of parking space on a university campus—a constant sore point for outside community participants.

The "Activities" part relates to the program elements needed to fulfill its mission (e.g., leadership training, planning, and teaching other kids, providing internships). In essence, this section describes what your program is going to do.

The "Outputs" part basically describes the direct products of program activities. These products include things like number of orientation and training sessions, number of leadership sessions, number of hours that service to other kids is provide, number of participants being served, and number of community partners involved with the program.

The final part relates to expected "Outcomes" (or goals) of the program (e.g., program commitment, confidence in leading, increased teaching skills, increased sensitivity to the welfare of others, improved behavior at school). Journals, rating forms, lesson plans, reflection and group meeting comments, evaluations from the younger children, talks with the leaders' teachers, counselors, principals, parents, and even bus drivers all provide viable information that should be commensurate with your program goals.

School records can also be a data source although we seldom rely on these. Of course, clearance from administrators, youth leaders, and parents is required to do this. As we said earlier, grades are not something we look at. However, attendance, office referrals, and counselor recommendations can help to augment other data sources. An important point here is that these types of data are reliant on the diligence of those who keep such records. We have found that "shoddy" record keeping is not uncommon in some schools. Computer retrieval systems are helpful to the extent in which student information is carefully entered into the data bank.

A helpful strategy in organizing these data sources is to develop an "assessment crosswalk" (O'Sullivan, 1993). Figure 12.6 shows an example of one that has been included in a recent proposal to the United Way. It is simply a visual representation of how each program goal is to be assessed. This format has become particularly useful in clarifying how each data source will be used. In addition, potential funding agencies find that the crosswalk provides a quick and interpretable snapshot of how assessment will be done.

PROGRAM MEASURES

PROGRAM GOALS	Adult Leader Journal	Leader Questionnaire	Assistant Ratings
Program Commitment	X		X
Responsible Leadership	X		X
Confidence in leading		X	
Teaching skillfulness	X	X	X

Figure 12.6   Evaluation crosswalk

Two other assessment strategies similar to the program outcome model, program theory evaluation (Rogers et al., 2000) and the theory of change approach (Vizzo et al., 2004), map not only the goals and outcomes of the program model but specific processes and strategies intended to achieve *each* goal. These approaches have the advantage of attribution: Specific program outcomes can be attributed to specific processes.

Use of Comparison Groups

At some point, you may feel compelled to use a comparison group to assess the true impact of your leadership program. In doing this, you try to compare your assessment measures to some comparable group of kids who are not involved with your leadership program—sometimes referred to as a control group. We believe that comparison groups have to be used with extreme caution. There is a basic assumption that members of a comparison group are identical across various characteristics except for their non-participation status in your leadership program. Moreover, controlled studies are governed by parametric assumptions, which are very difficult to adhere to in youth work. We therefore think that these assumptions are impossible to support in working with adolescents, especially if they come from underserved environments. It is also problematic when your participants voluntarily come to your program; that is, they choose to become part of your leadership program. Trying to control for grades, prior achievement, socioeconomic status, or other factors does not account for the obvious motivational levels of the leaders who elect to participate in your program or the urging they received from their teacher, principal, and perhaps parents to get involved. This is not to say that group comparisons cannot highlight possible causes. All we are saying is that making such comparisons must be insightful and pertinent to the true meaning of any differences found or not found.

Insights and Take-aways

There are many ways in which assessment can be handled in your program. Whatever way you choose, it will be important for each leader, regardless of the stage they are at, to benefit from the process. Unlike assessment in schools, the assessment of your leaders, yourself, and the program must serve more than just seeing if leaders know their stuff about leading others. They need to be able to live it, feel it, and share it with those around them. Here are some things from this chapter that will help to insure this happens.

- Assessment should not be treated as a separate part of your leadership program. Self ratings, self-reflection, group discussion, personal note-taking, adult-leader feedback are some of the assessment ways that can be interwoven within your program.
- Be clear as to how assessment can be used in your leadership program.
- An important first step in the assessment process is to determine if your program is doing what it was intended to do. Then you can follow up by assessing the youth leaders' development, your effectiveness as an adult leader, and various program goals.
- A program outcome model can be useful in assessing the overall operation of your program. The model guides you in determining resources, what the program intends to do, activities that fulfill program intentions, and the benefits derived from participation.
- Developing a program crosswalk is a simple way to interface sources of your assessment data with program goals.
- The person doing the assessment of your program should be familiar with its operation. This means that it should be done by either you or someone who has a clear understanding of your program.
- There are significant limitations in comparing your program participants to a "control" group. Therefore, using a comparison group in your assessment system has to be done with extreme caution.

13
Research on Youth Leadership Programs

To write it, it took three months; to conceive it—three minutes; to collect the data in it—all my life

—Unknown

In a way the previous chapter on assessment serves as a jumping off point for this chapter on research. We want to show the more formal ways responsibility-based youth leadership programs have been studied. Over the past two decades various research efforts have delved into the many facets of leadership programming. Many of these studies were generated by our past students while others came from university folk who, like us, ran values-based youth programs. It's important to note that while TPSR programs have a long history, formal research on TPSR and youth leadership, both published and unpublished, is relatively new. This is why knowing the types of studies, their designs, and outcomes will provide a clearer picture of the scope and character of program products. In turn, these products will provide important reference points for future research endeavors. The research in youth development (Benson, 2006; Halpern, 2003; McLaughlin, 2000; Wang & Gordon, 1994), the social sciences (e.g., deCharms, 1976; Erikson, 1988; Gilligan, 1982) and critical pedagogy (Friere, 1993; Rovegno & Kirk, 1995; McDonald et al., 2002) have all helped to inform us about evaluating youth serving programs.

In many cases, the approach to doing TPSR inquiry has cut across the grain of traditional positivistic research paradigms. Resistance to replicate the parent disciplines' methodologies has been buttressed by developing an alternative research strategy of our own called *service-bonded inquiry* (Hellison & Martinek, 1997, 2006b; Martinek, Hellison, & Walsh, 2004). By building upon ideas as opposed to just theory, service-bonded inquiry more effectively addresses the squirmy issues related to values acquisition and personal growth of young people.

Our approach to this chapter will be two dimensional. First, we describe the research that has pin-pointed outcomes related to the TPSR curriculum model itself. The second dimension focuses specifically on those studies that have looked at youth leadership programming per se. Keep in mind that while TPSR programming has been the "heart and soul" of leadership development, past studies reveal several benchmarks of development along the way. These benchmarks represent gateways to more advanced leadership experiences for children and youth.

TPSR Model Research—Here and Abroad

There have been well over thirty studies that have been conducted on Don's TPSR model. All of these studies have examined program impact on underserved or at-risk children and youth. Most of these studies, some of which we have mentioned in previous chapters, have taken place in the United States with several others conducted in Europe (Spain & Portugal) and Australia and New Zealand.

A number of TPSR studies have attempted to summarize findings by grouping the findings within a particular time period. One such study was conducted by Hellison and Walsh (2002) where twenty-six studies dating from 1978 to 2001 were analyzed and summarized. Twenty-one of the studies were case studies based on both qualitative and quantitative data. Both process and product measures were used across the twenty-six studies. Four research questions guided the analyses. Three attended to assessing TPSR outcome variables and one focused on program processes. Findings were also grouped into stronger and weaker evidence-based groups according to the number and quality of the studies and the nature of the findings. After data were analyzed and summarized they were compared to the principles underlying the TPSR model. Several conclusions that emerged show:

- Strong support for "Physical Activity as a potentially powerful vehicle for teaching life skills and values while at the same time promoting physical activity content learning."

- Strong support for "the overarching purpose [as helping] students take responsibility for their own well being and development and for contributing to the well-being of others."
- Variable support for program participants improving on the five goals (or levels) that help students focus on what to take responsibility for. Of the nineteen studies that investigated this question, fourteen reported self-control improvement and twelve reported effort improvement, but only eight showed self-direction improvement and only seven reported improvement in helping others. Perhaps most surprising, of the eleven studies that investigated transfer of these goals outside the gym, strong evidence of transfer was found for several goals. However, some evidence showed non-transfer as well. The two studies that examined cross-age teaching found strong support for the number of positive outcomes.
- Uneven support was found regarding the five themes that characterize daily practice and format as factors putting themes into practice. Exploration of the processes experienced by program participants turned up some evidence for interacting with a caring adult and having fun. However, the design of this review as well as most of the studies was not conducive to answering these process-oriented questions (Hellison & Martinek, 2006b, p. 618).

Individual Program Studies

Several of the studies in Hellison and Walsh's review plus others that followed originated from either the Chicago or Greensboro TPSR programs. One of the early studies out of the Chicago program (Debusk & Hellison, 1989) used a case study approach to examine program impact of ten 4th grade boys. The program which utilized the TPSR model ran for approximately six weeks. The participants were referred to the program by school officials. Over a hundred handwritten pages were transcribed from responses from pre- and post-interviews of each club member. Office referrals and teacher-research field notes served as another data source. The data suggested that the responsibility model helped the students become aware of the self-responsibility concepts and incorporate the values of TPSR in their everyday lives. Affective changes were also found in the program. However, none of these changes occurred in the classroom setting.

In a later study by Don and Paul Wright (Hellison & Wright, 2003), TPSR post-program impact after a nine-year period of participation was examined. Club members' attendance over the nine-year period and various qualitative measures constituted the data base of the study. Results of the study showed that the program retention rates surpassed the average drop-out rate of inner city youth in other extended day programs. Other data showed that personal and social responsibility improvements were evident—a consequence of their participation in the program. Interestingly, many of the students also indicated that having a caring and respectful leader in their program was a big factor for them to attend—a factor that has been emphasized several times in this book.

In another longitudinal study, Tammy Schilling (2001) evaluated "veteran" club members from the Project Effort program in Greensboro. Since the program started with students in an elementary school in an underserved area of the city, the program staff was interested in finding out why club members stayed in the program over multiple years. Therefore, she wanted to determine factors that influenced their continued involvement and commitment over a five-year period. Using a case study approach she interviewed (individual & focus) and applied a "card sorting" strategy with seven participants. She wanted to ask them about the barriers (e.g., gang involvement, school experiences) to program commitment and compare their own and the program staff's perceptions of their commitment levels. Based on the responses from the interviews, themes were determined (e.g., learning activities, having a mentor) and placed on an index card. Each participant was then asked to "sort" the cards according to their importance to keeping them involved in the sport program. This procedure allowed Schilling to look across all participants to see what aspects of the program were least or more important.

Following content analysis she found that their involvement in the program was influenced by variation in activities, having fun, having a voice in how the program runs, staying out of trouble, and having program goals. The participants also stayed with the program across multiple years because of relationships with the staff and other club members (see chapter 9).

Wright and White (2003) focused their attention on TPSR and special needs children. They looked at program impact on cerebral palsy children who participated in a modified version of a TPSR sport program. Adapting to the nuances of a special education population of kids, the researchers tested the philosophical notions of a TPSR program. The sources of the data were medical records of the kids, field notes, and interviews of the participants' physicians, therapists, and parents. The researchers found the program increased the participants' sense of ability, produced positive feelings about the program, and generated healthy social interactions among other participants and staff.

Throughout this book we have expressed concern about club members' inability to apply the responsibility values they learn in the club to other places in their lives. This problematic area of youth development programming, especially during those early experiences in our sport clubs, has certainly been acknowledged through focused inquiries into the barriers affecting value transfer.

One of these studies was conducted by Tom and two of his doctoral students—Tammy Schilling and Dennis Johnson (Martinek, Schilling, & Johnson, 1999) in the Project Effort program. They wanted to see whether the values and goals of the club, once learned, could be applied back at their school. To assist in the transfer of the goals mentors were matched with each club member. The general goal of the mentor component was to get youngsters to transfer the goal-setting strategies and values acquired in the clubs to the classroom and home setting. To do this, graduate and undergraduate students and the researchers spent an additional two hours each week working with a student at the school site.

Mentors continually reinforced the importance of trying hard in the face of challenges (TPSR level two). Monitoring and encouragement were important roles played by the mentors during the goal-setting process. The idea was to make the child believe that trying hard was one of the reasons for success—gaining personal control over their behavior and academic work. This included providing alternative strategies for approaching learning tasks or behavioral difficulties in the classroom and gymnasium.

Each student had their own portfolio which included various types of data. Data sources included mentor journal entries, staff observations, and teacher ratings of classroom performance. A data matrix was developed from these data (Demos, 1989; Van Tulder, Van der Vegt, & Veenman, 1993) to organize and interpret how each club member was meeting the goals of the program. The matrix also allowed the evaluators to see how well the club members transferred the values and goals of the TPSR model to the classroom setting.

The results showed that the youngsters were able to acquire a degree of persistence at learning tasks in the gym and the classroom. Their ability to set goals and respect others in the gym also appeared to be present during the program. The club members, however, struggled to transfer some of the TPSR values to their classroom. For example, incidences of self control, respect, and caring for others were not as high in the classroom as in the gym. The evaluators felt this inability to transfer the values of the gym to the classroom also partially reflected a lack of ownership in the values of the club.

As a follow up to this study, Tom, Dan McLaughlin, and Tammy Schilling (1999) looked at actual school performance measures of Project Effort participants. These measures included nine-week grades, recorded teacher reprimands, and office referrals obtained from school records. Mentor journal entries were once again used as a data source. The teachers were also asked to comment on how hard the kids tried in their classroom work. Overall improvement in students' engagement in class work along with increases in grade point average and decreases in reprimands and office referrals were reported. Teachers also noted that barriers to preventing positive impact for some of the students were home and neighborhood factors (e.g., unstable caregiver, gangs, and drug dealing).

A more recent study by Okseon Lee and Tom looked further into the cultural barriers of the school that prevented transfer from occurring (Lee & Martinek, 2009). Considering the limitations in transfer studies, one important area of research that needed to be examined was children's lives both in an after-school program and in school. One important premise was foundational to the study. That premise was that since the TPSR model is a values-based model (Hellison, 2003), how program values were perceived and communicated in both the physical activity program and participants' school could be a critical factor in connecting the two. Therefore, the purpose of the study was to investigate and analyze the culture of the Project Effort Sport Club along with the club members' school. The school culture was defined according to its characterizations, values, norms, and behaviors.

Five children who had at least one full semester of participation in the program were in the study. Data were collected from participants' individual interviews and observations of their involvement both at school and in Project Effort. Findings revealed that there was a clear difference in the participants' perceptions of atmosphere between the after-school program and their school. Based on the interview data of the students, cultural differences were due, in large part, to the test-centeredness of the school. That is, achieving high test scores was perceived as a top priority for both students and teachers in the wake of the enactment of the law, "No Child Left Behind." The major academic task in the school was test preparation, which required individual work rather than cooperative work. In this context, students defined self-direction as "mind your own business" and focused on their own test scores rather than helping other people. The inconsistent communication of values between Project Effort and the school setting worked as structural borders which were created by "differences in expectations for how schools as institutions should operate" (Phelan, Davidson, & Yu, 1998, p. 13).

A higher priority was also placed on the values of control and achievement—two expectations of the school system. School norms were enforced strongly by rewards and punishments (e.g., silent lunch, no recess). Because Project Effort participants perceived their sport club and school settings as very different from one another, psychosocial borders or barriers (e.g., lack of control, a sense of insecurity) were created in their school life. These were definite sources of conflict for the students and worked as negative forces in transferring program TPSR values from the sport club to the school setting.

International Studies

On the international front, TPSR programming and the transfer issue have been evaluated several ways. For example, Gordon's (2005) six-month study of high school physical education classes in New Zealand looked at how TPSR affected class climate, behavior, detention rate, and goal setting. Daily teacher notations of student behaviors, self-reflection journals, and interviews of teachers all served as the data sources for the investigation. The results showed significant improvement in class atmosphere and relations between students and teachers. Also, some evidence of transferring these qualities to the classroom setting was reported.

Amparo Escarti and her research team (Escarti, Pascual, & Gutierrez, 2005) at the University of Valencia in Spain summarized a number of studies that focused TPSR interventions. One was on underserved youth in an after-school coaching club (see Hellison, Cutforth, Kallusky, Martinek, Parker, & Stiehl, 2000). The other was by Pedro Martin of Madrid University, who implemented TPSR with low income youth and reported positive changes in their values within the physical education setting. As with previous studies, however, the ability to apply the values outside of the gym was once again thwarted. Frustration with the social and economic barriers to apply these values outside the gym was found to be enormous challenges.

And there is Portuguese researcher and teacher, Leonor Reguieras, of the University of Porto. Her present work (Reguieras, 2008) taps into a much needed area of inquiry in youth development programming. Her work veers away from the transfer issue by focusing on adult leadership characterizations of values, goals, and motivations. Interestingly, little research has been done on those individuals who have provided distinct leadership in youth sport programming. So much of the research has looked solely at participant outcomes. While these participant by-products serve useful purposes in program development, it would seem as important (or even more important) to know the qualities and motives of those who develop and run youth development programs.

More specifically, Leonor is exploring the values, styles, and missions of selected leaders in youth sport development programs. By contrasting and comparing their views of youth development programming, she is able to uncover some of the unique and common features that drive their work with an assessment of the youngsters with whom they work. Relationship building is also a focal point of her inquiry. That is, knowing the requirements for good communication with and understanding of young people are additional focal points of her inquiry. Through individual in-depth interviews with six national and international leaders in youth sport programming, she was able to show that while there were some unique differences among the leaders, features like focusing on kids' strengths, relationship building, and having a clear set of values were common themes among the leaders. Another dimension of her work also described each leader's expectations for program impact. Most of the leaders indicated that there is an important balance that has to be made between the challenges that kids face and what the program can deliver in addressing them.

Youth Leadership Program Studies

Because TPSR sport programs have provided the stepping stones to advance leadership experiences, investigations into their efficacy have become prevalent within the last several years. Uncovering the products of youth leadership development have allowed us to realize the large and small benefits of programming that evolve from stage three and four programming. As studies continue to emerge, we will be able to tap into a richer network of ideas for elevating young people's desire to contribute to their community. For this to occur it is important to pay attention to those past and present studies that have attempted to extricate factors the reveal good and not so good things about program impact.

In chapter 12, we referred to several studies that relied on various data sources. One of these studies was conducted by Nick Cutforth and

Karen Puckett (1999). They evaluated Chicago's Apprentice Teachers Program which was designed for eleven high school kids who were given the responsibility to teach forty nine-year-olds from a nearby public housing community. The program ran four days per week over a five-week period. Both quantitative and qualitative methods were used to obtain information about the experiences in this sport camp. Both evaluators used informal observations, entries from a personal journal kept by the program director, and interview responses from the director and apprentice teachers before and after the program as the main data sources. In addition, the director took attendance and graded (i.e., A, B, C, D, F) the apprentice teachers' effectiveness.

An important aspect of this evaluation was that Nick and Karen knew the apprentice teachers and had worked with them in previous years in the Coaching Club. Their familiarity with the teachers created open and honest discussions during interview sessions, thus enhancing the believability of the data.

The data showed that eight of the apprentice teachers' attendance was steady. The greatest challenge, however, was to make the teachers aware of their leadership role, particularly in taking charge of their sessions. Some teachers were organized and focused on teaching sport skills and keeping the children motivated to learn. However, there were others who needed close supervision throughout the camp experience in order to make sure they were prepared to teach. Others simply needed confirmation that they were on the right track. Their constant struggles with managing off-task behavior of the children indicated that some training was needed at the front end of the program. They also had a difficult time in teaching basic sport skills. Nick and Karen also felt it was necessary to dilute the competitive nature of the apprentice teachers so that the less skilled kids would not be excluded from game play.

As with most evaluation schemes this particular study provided great baseline data for future inquiry of the impact of the Apprentice Teacher Program. The evaluation also showed that the teachers' awareness of the importance of helping others could be elevated through this type of program. The apprentice teachers' eagerness to be part of next year's program was apparent for all the young teachers. This further suggests that such commitment may be the beginnings of creating a vision of an alternative future for themselves.

In another study on youth leadership development (Martinek, Schilling, & Hellison, 2006), the researchers looked at how youth leaders advanced in their leadership skills throughout a program.

Similar to the other studies reported thus far, qualitative and quantitative data sources (i.e., interviews, journal entries, and field notes) were once again analyzed. Using a case study approach, four youth leaders from the Greensboro Youth Leader Corps program were profiled according to their responses to their leadership experiences and subsequent growth. Each leader was profiled along a continuum of leadership qualities that were based on learned helplessness (Martinek & Griffith, 1993) and moral development theories (Burns, 1978; Gilligan, 1982; Kohlberg, 1971). Four stages of leadership development were differentiated through each leader's reasons for leading others. These reasons ranged from leading because of personal needs (e.g., wanting to be with friends) to those that were genuinely focused on meeting the needs of others. As previously underscored throughout this book, these stages were also found to be fluid; that is, they fluctuated considerably due to outside circumstances experienced by each of the leaders (Hellison & Martinek, 2006b). These data also gave guidance for the adult leader to prepare and adjust for the uncertainties associated in developing young people into caring and compassionate leaders.

Earlier we described the factors that sustain participants' involvement in Greensboro's Project Effort Sport Club (Schilling, 1999). In a rare follow-up study by Tammy Schilling, Tom Martinek, and Sarah Carson (2007), an attempt was made to find out reasons for the youth leaders' sustained involvement in the Youth Leader Corps program. Twelve adolescents from Schilling's original study were included in the study. The barriers that challenged their commitment were also identified. Individual interviews revealed program-related barriers that included logistics, structure, and relationships, and personal-related barriers which included perceived alternatives, personal characteristics, and "real-life" responsibilities. Similar to the 2001 study, antecedents were grouped under program environment, program structure, relationships, and personal characteristics. Participants also described outcomes in terms of behavior and emotional involvement related to program commitment. For example, trying hard, sticking with it, enjoying the chance to lead, motivation, and regular attendance reflected attributes of program commitment for them.

A final study deals with finding out what leaders do after they leave the Youth Leader Corps. We have often emphasized the importance of evaluating the latent effects of leadership program participation. Chapter 8 (Self-actualized Leadership) underscores the importance of moving young people to a position in their lives where they begin to acquire clarity of vision and purpose. Responsible parenting, holding down a job that has meaning, imparting important life skills to others, and envisioning even greater possibilities for oneself are the tangibles and intangibles of this process.

In a study by Tammy Schilling (2008) the story of Tasha, a past Youth Leaders Corps member was told. Tasha graduated from high school, eventually got married, acquired several jobs, pursued post-secondary education, and had three children in the process. From interviews of Tasha and her mom, the researcher crafted a telling story of how past experiences in the Youth Leader Corps intersected with challenges related to social identity, disconnection from her primary caregiver, and teenage pregnancy. Love for her kids, self-confidence in facing challenges, ability to distance herself from a stressful home environment, and a strong sense of social and moral maturity were essential protective mechanisms that helped her grapple with her life challenges. The story uncovers the key adaptive factors that played a role in her life. Several of these were connected to program membership and its empowering atmosphere. For example, opportunity to make decisions and demonstrate responsible leadership ability in the program, and having a strong connection to the program leader all served as resiliency building agents. In the end, along with her strong personality traits, past program involvement had, in part, maintained the impulse for self discovery and commitment to help others (her own children).

Insights and Take-aways

This chapter has provided a number of studies connected to TPSR values based sport programs and leadership opportunities for young people. These studies and future ones will continue to create modifications in our approach to both programs. That's why continual study of these programs will be needed regardless of the methodologies and data sources called upon to accomplish the task. Here are some things that we hope will guide future research efforts:

- Research on youth leadership programming is at its beginning stages in the area of sport. Creative as well as traditional forms of inquiry (i.e., mixed methods) will be needed to sustain vigorous research activity. One of these alternative forms, *service-bonded inquiry*, effectively addresses those questions related to value and relational outcomes of youth programming.

- TPSR studies have included those that focus on programs that serve as precursors to more advanced leadership development programs. These studies have been done at both national and international levels, thus providing cross-cultural representation of products and methodologies.
- Transfer studies have shown some modest positive outcomes. However, these studies show that barriers to effective application of program values continue to be related to poverty and the school culture.
- Adult leaders' qualities remain an unexplored area of inquiry. More needs to be done in this area so the professional training in youth development can be further enhanced.
- Many of the studies on youth leadership programming have been connected to process and product variables (teaching effectiveness, attendance, commitment, and values orientation). Some have begun looking at the impact on past youth leaders' later life circumstances.

14
Making It Happen

My goal is to be morally strong, and I think I have failed at every turn. Every now and then I have a moment where it's a little something.

—Ken Howard, "The White Shadow"

If you are thinking of starting your own leadership program, no doubt the first question that will loom from your deliberation is "When and how do I get started?" The answer to the first part of that question is that there is no special time to begin... so do it NOW! Martin Luther King once said, "The time is always right to do the right thing." Begin creating your own vision as to how you want your program to look. Remember this is your program—not ours. So think of how your vision will result in a great leadership program.

The answer to the second part of the question is a little more complex. Your circumstance will have a lot to do with how your program will evolve. Earlier we talk about the importance of having resources, support, and community connections. These factors will impact on how you proceed with program planning and so they must be carefully assessed before you begin. However, we believe there are several strategies that will help to insure a good start for your program, regardless of your situation:

- Start small
- Connect with resources
- Be prepared for challenges
- Don't forget your values

Start Small

Several years ago a close colleague of ours at another university was thinking of starting a leadership program with several schools. However, she was worried about the time it would require to organize and run the program. She was afraid that with everything else to do, the possibility of fitting it into her schedule seemed doubtful. Our best advice to her (and you) was to start small and try not to change the world. When both of us started our sport and leadership programs we started with small numbers of kids and a tight time schedule. We wanted to try out our ideas in one program that we thought we could handle. One day a week with one group made the start up tenable. As a university faculty, especially if you are untenured, the concept of "less is more" must guide planning as you begin your program. Balancing the time between academic and program demands must be carefully considered. Otherwise, the quality of your work in both contexts will suffer.

If you're working in a community youth program like the Boys and Girls Club or recreation program, it is also wise to start with a small group of kids. This is especially important when working on the early stages of leadership experiences. Since community programs will either have kids who come often or time to time, it is best to select those kids who attend on a regular basis. You can work with them early, advancing them through the stages of development and eventually have them assist in teaching or mentoring the other kids in the club.

Nsandjo Macha, a director of a Boys and Girls Club in Greensboro, would select some of the older kids in the club to help with certain activities involving the younger club members. He then began working with them on Saturdays to work on more advanced leadership skill (Stages 1 and 2) so they could eventually help teach sport skills (and life skills) to smaller groups of kids during the regular club times. Over time his "new staff" was able to provide the much needed relief for his overstretched staff.

Similarly, Stephanie Baldwin, an Americorps volunteer has developed her own version of a "Leadership Club." Stephanie runs a youth and family service program in one of Greensboro's immigrant public housing communities. She was also able to attend one of Tom's workshops and became a frequent visitor to his Youth Leader Corps program. Using some of the concepts and ideas borrowed from the Youth Leader Corps program she began a small leadership program with a few of the high school residents. Stephanie's leaders were not only positive contributors to the Americorps mission but became positive role models for the younger children in their own community.

And then there is James Hollins who grabbed a bunch of ideas from a visitation to Chicago's leadership program. Several years later he is still using those ideas in his work with low income youth in Chicago. For those of you who work in school programs, the "less is more" theme is equally important. You can start with one class, select a small group of kids, and meet with them outside of the regular class times. Kim Berg's Breakfast Club and Nick Cutforth's Energizer Clubs (see chapter 7) were good examples of how older and more responsible kids in your school can be trained and ready to help teach some of your younger kids either during the school day or as part of a special before- and after-school program (Cutforth, 1997).

One cautionary note: Start with the first stage of youth leadership development—Learning to Take Responsibility—before thinking of implementing the other stages. Progression is a key here and starting small means starting at the beginning before adding on the other stages of leadership experiences. Work with the first stage, play with it, reflect on it, play with it again, and so on. When you feel comfortable with what you have accomplished then move on to more advanced stages. Keeping it small and following with progressively small steps is part of the developmental process.

Connect with Resources

Early on we talked about the importance of securing resources for your program. Resources can take the shape of many things. And, their availability and access can vary depending on the context in which the program will operate (e.g., university, school, Boys and Girls Club, YMCA). One of these resources is space. Regardless of where you work (i.e., university, school, community-based program) there will be many factors that impact space availability. Obviously, one of these factors is simply having limited space for physical activity (e.g., no gym). A lunch room, hallway, school stage, and arts and craft room are some examples of spaces that limit physical activity programming. Other factors are those programs that require shared space at your center or school (e.g., special community events, other sport programs). For example, in Chicago the pressure on increasing test scores created by the "No Child Left Behind" has caused space to become scarce for running after-school programs. Consequently, gym and cafeteria space have been lost to academic tutorial programs.

In Greensboro's campus-based program, the scheduling of athletic practice, summer sport camps, and university courses determines which day and times the Youth Leader Corps Program can be offered. Likewise, school- and community-based programs face the similar scheduling considerations although we have found that there seems to be a little more scheduling flexibility within these programs.

Another important resource is your community partnerships—something emphasized in chapters 7 and 8. Because kids already attend community-based and school programs, you have a "ready made" access to this resource. However, university programs will rely heavily on the faculty member's ability to establish ties to community agencies (see Walsh, 2002) in order to get students to participate. Likewise, the successful implementation of stages three and four experiences will heavily depend on making connections to community partners for teaching and internship experiences. Keep in mind, however, that securing these partnerships are further down the road in your program considerations and should not be a prerequisite to getting started.

A final, less tangible but most important source, will be your perseverance. As excited as you may be about doing this kind of work, you must be prepared for those ups and downs due to kids' behavior and attitudes and colleague support. To test your readiness for this work it is helpful to ask yourself: "Why should I do this work?" In response to this question we are reminded of Mahatma Gandhi's insightful proclamation: "You must be the change you wish to see in the world." These words reflect the spirit that you must have to get kids where you want them to be. Each youngster brings into the program circumstances and daily experiences unique in severity and scope. Young leaders will also bring in various levels of adaptability that has allowed them to navigate through a social system fraught with economic, social, and geographic barriers (Hellison et al., 2000). Racism, poverty, and societal indifference are common denominators among underserved youth and will not disappear. You will also find that these barriers become the unwanted companions of your work, thus making it far from being easy. But, what will keep you going is the excitement of being in a position to have the opportunity to do something for your kids—to enable them to successfully confront these problems.

Another response to the question "Why should I do this work?" is that young people need something that an adult person—you—possess: experience, status, abilities, and hopefully, a caring attitude.

Consequently, your status is appreciably elevated beyond the level of an administrator or teacher. You now become a leader and role model for them. Such status crystallizes your relationships with them in a way that will give you enormous responsibility. If a youth leadership program is to be successful at all, it must be seen as a relationship between you and the young people with whom you work. It cannot turn into a program that is merely developed and administered (Swinehart, 1990).

A third response to the question "Why should I do this work?" is one that is often heard from youth workers: "I want to make a difference!" As an adult leader, you can make a difference, but it will be a difference that is hard to predict. William Damon often finds in his work as a child psychologist that young people must discover their own unique purposes, out of their own interests and values (Damon, 2008). You, as an adult leader, can only guide them by shaping discoveries and creating a culture around them that engages them in ways that help them and those they lead to become responsible people. It is applying Myles Horton's "two-eyed" theory—keeping one eye on where kids are and one eye on where they can be (see Littky, 2004). This also means that *you cannot* provide a ready-made purpose to a young leader's life. What you can do, however, is get to know them for who they are, inspire them to have a vision of a possible future, and cultivate their will to search, and explore possible pathways to future goals.

A final response to the question "Why should I do this work?" is simply "change is needed!" For us, it is time to change the effects of the self-fulfilling prophecy created by low expectations of teachers, administrators, and, even parents. For too long many young people, especially those who are underserved, have been crippled by the "you can't" messages thrown at them throughout their lives. Thinking outside the box in terms of how we can effectively get kids to see themselves as leaders will be a huge challenge. Negative self-perceptions are hard to change. That is why reflection, decision making, and power sharing are so crucial in helping kids discover what they can be. Sometimes the changes are small ones. Sometimes they need to be big ones. But whatever their size they all translate into possibilities for fostering aspirations, finding purpose, and regaining membership in their community.

Prepare for Challenges

In the early part of your program expect to confront obstacles. Some of these translate into leaders' misunderstanding of what the program is all about. Additionally, challenges can be seen in the leaders' inability to focus on their leadership roles. Keep in mind that most, if not all leaders, have certain needs, none of which can be ignored by you. Those leaders whose needs are all-consuming will respond much differently to their leadership roles than those who are able to place needs aside for the sake of leading others.

A good example of how needs-based leaders can back away from their leadership roles was evident with two of Greensboro's leaders, Otis and Nicole. One day they were nowhere to be found as their children filed into the gym; their teaching area was not set up. One of the leaders told the adult leader (Tom) to look in a small closet outside the gym. When the closet door swung open he discovered Otis and Nicole embraced in a "romantic interlude." Obviously, the need to be prepared for their kids took a back seat to their need to be together!

On the other hand, there was Derek, who exemplified a more advanced stage of leadership behavior. Derek always came early, set up his teaching area, and even greeted the children as they came into the gym! His needs, although still a part of his life, were set aside for the welfare of his kids.

You will also be confronted with making tough decisions due to circumstances that suddenly emerge. Having to make these decisions can take their toll and often make you second guess if this is the right thing to do. For example, what do you do when one of your leaders is suspended from school? Do you let the leader still participate? If not, who will be responsible for teaching his/her group of kids? Or, if you let the leader continue to participate, what can you do or say that reinforces the consequence for screwing up in school? Or what do you do when a leader experiences a personal set back, like the death of a friend or family member? When and how do you effectively address the issue with the leader so that he or she can stay on track? Our recommendation is to not waver and persevere in addressing these problems. This means that determination, problem solving, and tough decision-making will be key factors in keeping you on track.

James Kallusky had a great way of persevering over such obstacles. He kept track of what he called "daily private victories." They are those small incidents that occur in your program that give you faith that things are working (Hellison et al., 2000). These events can be as small as a leader that continually comes on time or volunteers to gather some of the equipment left out from a session or it can be when one the children tell you how much they enjoyed working with her leader. Don't underestimate the importance of recognizing these small victories. They will rebuff those feelings of self doubt that so often creep in when facing the challenges of being an adult leader. So "not giving up" is the message here; it needs to be part of your mindset. If you give up on your program, you give up on kids. As James Kallusky poignantly stated, "Good adult leaders occasionally become heroes, and there is nothing wrong with that" (p. 209).

Don't Forget Your Values

Your values will play a huge role in what your program will look like. We have stressed this several times throughout our book. Our take on leadership embraces a set of values based on the TPSR framework. We believe they are important for kids to absorb, practice, and internalize. For us, they form the foundation for elevating their need to become caring and compassionate leaders. At the same time, for those of you who are unfamiliar to TPSR, we can only hope that you embrace a set of values that will reflect the spirit of TPSR. We have tried to thread them throughout this book and trust that they will remain steadfast as you plan and implement your leadership program.

As you prepare to meet the challenges ahead of you, it will be helpful to think of your program as a living organism. Like any living organism, a good program has to change continuously and be ready to change at any moment. If your program is to be successful, it must continually look at itself, question what it does, and make adjustments when necessary (Littky, 2004). When young leaders walk out from your program you need to ask: What do you want them to take with them? Your answer should be: You can only plant seeds that will bear the fruit of your values that shape their lives in a positive way. In the end, your values and commitment to teaching them will have an enormous pay-off for your leaders—they will become more self directed and caring people.

A Final Thought

Clearly the path that young people take to developing their leadership potential will be circuitous and unpredictable. Frustration, success, and failure will all be part of the journey for your leaders and you! Their leadership development will not only depend on your leadership, but where they find themselves in life. If we are to alter the stereotypic perceptions of what and who leaders should be, young people need to become keenly aware of their leadership potential. This will especially true for those of you who work with kids who have been marginalized from the mainstream. In short, making all kids positive contributors to their community is what it is all about. The ideas presented in this book are just a few of examples of ways in which you can awaken young people to this realization. So your support will be crucial here. It will not only help them find and follow their path as leaders but affirm their importance to their community.

Insights and Take-aways

In figuring out the best way to bring closure to this book we are reminded that there is never any real closure to this work. We are fully aware that there are those of you who may not be quite sure how to get started in this work. This chapter focuses on bringing clarity to how to begin this journey of leadership development and how you can make it happen.

- In starting a leadership program you need to consider *your* circumstance, *your* values, *your* emotional investment, and *your* resource support. They will all determine where you want to go with your program and the pathway that will get you there.
- "Starting small" means begin with low numbers and a clear understanding of resource availability. It also means forming experiences from the beginning stages of leadership development. Progression must be at the forefront of planning.
- Connecting with resources, preparing for challenges, and holding onto your values are key factors to consider with planning a youth leadership program.
- Your program will continually evolve as you examine and reexamine what is working and whether the fidelity of TPSR values are maintained throughout the development of your youth leaders. Challenges that come your way will force you to make the changes needed to insure positive and lasting program outcomes.

Epilogue

Three Questions

I feel like I am respected because children listen to what I am saying and they take it to heart.

—Youth Leader Corps member

Leadership has become a buzz word in educational and youth development circles. Youth workers, teachers, coaches, curriculum specialists, and professional development university faculty face increasing advocacy for more and better youth development programs. We have mentioned some of these specific programs, but our focus has been on our own work with kids and that of our former students and likeminded colleagues.

To wrap up our case for youth leadership development, we address three overarching questions:

- Why do we think our approach is important?
- Why do we think it works?
- How fallible are our values and ideas?

Why Do We Think Our Approach Is Important?

Our work with kids is driven by a few core values as well as our experiences in urban youth program development. As one teacher told us when asked if our approach was working with his kids, he replied "No, but it will!" He so believed in the underlying values that he was determined to outlast the critics, balky kids, and a doubtful administrator. His patience paid off as teachers began to report positive changes in attitude and behavior, and referrals to the office declined. Our commitment to a set of values and beliefs outweighs whatever setbacks we experience.

At the same time, experience has taught us to constantly adjust our pedagogical practices, to go more slowly or progress at a faster pace, to modify some of our ideas, to individualize in order to meet students where they are. These kinds of bumps in the road have not only left a mark on our work but have caused us to feel very humble in sharing our ideas with others. Contexts also differ, as do professional responsibilities, limiting the reach of our own experiences. A school functions differently from a community youth organization, and both differ from programs sponsored by police and juvenile justice systems. Teachers, coaches, youth workers, and other related professionals face different issues such as the role of school rules, unique organized sport issues (e.g., how important should winning be?), and the need to recruit and retain kids who attend voluntarily.

Our approach uses physical activities as more than a "hook" (Hartmann, 2003; Hirsch, 2005). It embeds basic youth development principles such as leadership in the physical activity content (Hamilton & Hamilton, 2004). It is leadership by doing, by trial-and-error learning, not for future leadership but leadership right now, first with peers, then with younger kids, and finally in the community.

Moreover, our approach emphasizes servant leadership (Komives et al., 1998) rather than a top down dictatorship in which the leader tells followers what to do, when to do it, and how well or poorly they are doing it. Followers' only task is to do it! Servant leadership attempts to address the needs of the kids, to serve the kids. We also emphasize that all kids can be leaders, not just athletes, not just the most outgoing, not just the "favorites" of the adult leaders. Our leadership approach stresses caring and compassionate leadership which can help, as Outward Bound founder Kurt Hahn so succinctly put it, "make the brave gentle and the gentle brave" (Richards, 1982). It's not an easy road for youth leaders. "To be an effective leader, kids have to strive against external forces" (deCharms, 1986), not only those forces impinging on them but on their peers as well. That means, for example, not acting "cool" or tough despite peer pressure to do so. To top it off, we emphasize intrinsic rewards in a sport culture (as well as larger culture) that emphasizes extrinsic rewards such as trophies and other tangible awards, promotion of winners, and celebrations of the physically elite. We've discovered that all of our alternatives to common practice are possible, but kids must practice them and gradually "buy in" to their meaning and worth. The buy-in does not always come first! One of our students who was with us from fifth grade through high school graduation said that he had no idea what we were talking about for the first three years, despite being one of our best leaders! He just stuck around for the basketball and the relationships. He certainly had the program leader (one of us) fooled!

One more point on why we think this work is important. While all kids can be leaders and would benefit from the experience, our focus for over fifty years (combining our individual years of experience) has been to try to level the playing field to some extent for high-needs kids who live in underserved communities, are often seen as troublemakers, and sometimes have run-ins with the juvenile justice system. That's our niche, so this book is slanted in that direction. At the same time, everything we have shared also applies to more affluent youth who have their own set of problems, including drugs, teen pregnancy, suicide, and homicide. But regardless of the changing tone of many affluent communities, leadership training is also needed for those kids whose circumstances privilege them. Right or wrong, they are the most likely candidates for future civic and educational leadership positions, and many of them could use a strong dose of *responsible* servant leadership.

Why Do We Think It Works?

We have devoted a chapter to assessment in order to share some evaluation tools, but our answer to this question extends beyond that chapter. Evidence certainly matters, especially to funders and academics, but in this book we have shared a number of anecdotal examples portraying kids who have benefited from leadership experience. These kinds of experiences are powerful evidence for us, whether or not they are recognized by research methodologists. Fortunately, qualitative research methodologies have broadened considerably since Lincoln and Guba's (1985) views had top billing. This has also given service-bonded inquiry (Martinek, Hellison, & Walsh, 2004) some solid footing and scope for doing meaningful program evaluation.

Throughout our careers, we tried to practice a multidimensional trial-and-error approach (with lots of errors), to be adult role models who purposely try to develop meaningful relationships with individual kids, and to implement a specific framework based on combining TPSR with four stages of leadership, all aimed at promoting youth leadership. We think these strategies are likely to have a greater impact than any one strategy acting alone. Trial-and-error necessarily accompanies efforts to put new ideas into practice. Being a relational role model supports University of Regina professor Nick Forsberg's observation that TPSR is not a way of teaching, "it's a way of being" (personal communication). Our leadership stages—by providing a progression that begins with leadership awareness, advances to peer and cross-age teaching and coaching, and culminates in community leadership experiences—offer a structure for planning and assessing kids' progress as leaders.

In a broader sense, the recognizing of physical activity as a legitimate youth development approach, not just as a "hook" but as a legitimate training ground for leadership, further supports our approach (Perkins & Menestrel, 2007). However, none of these arguments hold up for programs that do not possess fidelity in relation to the leadership model being employed. For example, in our work, responsibility does not mean, "If you do what I say you are being responsible," nor does it mean that anything goes. It means doing as one must, not as one pleases (deCharms, 1986). These misinterpretations reflect an absence of fidelity to the leadership approach we are advocating and therefore do not represent what we have been advocating.

How Fallible Is Our Approach?

We have already confessed that our work is based on a blend of values, beliefs, and experiences with kids, making it "by definition" fallible. But no matter how much evidence is piled up in support of a particular approach to leadership or any other youth development idea, the believing and cherishing of the adult leader cannot be ignored (Greene, 1986). Research strongly supports the influence of an adult leader's professional values in the adoption of any program model, regardless of the strength of evidence of its effectiveness (Coburn, 2003; Lytle, 2002).

Moreover, rather than appealing to the research that supports our approach (e.g., Hellison & Walsh, 2002), we have pointed out that these are just ideas. And we've stated that our youth leadership developmental framework is still evolving. We've also recognized other promising sport-based youth leadership programs, such as Charlie Tribe's Sports 37 program in the Chicago Park District.

We have shared personal examples of our leadership work in after-school and physical education programs, but contexts differ, as do professional roles as we have already noted, and we have not had experiences in all of them. In closing, however, we should at least mention Walt Kelly's TPSR-based high school varsity football program (Hellison, 2003) and an early TPSR-based high school varsity wrestling program coached by one of us (Hellison, 1980). Neither of these organized sport programs benefited from the leadership stages, but they did attempt to promote leadership roles on the team in the spirit of this book.

Since we are sharing our fallibility here, it is fitting to close with an old quote that one of us has cited twice before (Hellison, 1978, 2003). It is still true, so we invite you to join us for a walk "in the mud."

Ideas are clean
I can take them out and look at them.
They fit nicely into books.
They lead me down the narrow way.
And in the morning they are there.
Ideas are straight.
But the world is round
And a messy mortal is my friend.
Come walk with me in the mud.

(Prather, 1970)

Appendix I

Content of Leader Notebook Samples

YOUTH LEADER CORPS PROGRAM DATES
Spring Semester
January 19 (training), 26 (training)
February 2, 9, 16, 23
March 2, 16, 23, 30
April 6, 20, 27

SPORT CLUB ROUTINE
Practice time
Large Group meeting
Small group work
Small game with home group
Large group meeting
Dismissal
Leader/assistant meeting
Planning
Dinner

YOUTH LEADER CORPS
Leader Plans/Comments

Lesson Activity:

Leadership Rating:	All World	Good	Fair	Not So Good	Ugh!
Being ready	5	4	3	2	1
Being with it	5	4	3	2	1
Being enthused	5	4	3	2	1
Being a role model	5	4	3	2	1

Leader Comments:
Assistant Comments:

THE FOUR B's

Be ready
Be enthused
Be with it
Be a role model

YOUTH LEADER CORPS PERSONAL AND SOCIAL RESPONSIBILITY MODEL

Level 1: RESPECT for the rights and feelings of others
- Self control
- Cooperation/teamwork
- Peaceful conflict resolution

Level 2: EFFORT
- On task
- Trying your best
- Defining personal success

Level 3: SELF DIRECTION
- Goal setting
- Setting personal challenges
- Working on your own

Level 4: HELPING AND LEADING OTHERS
- Concern for group welfare
- Being sensitive and responsive
- Caring for others

Level 5: TAKING "IT" OUTSIDE THE GYM
- Home
- School
- Neighborhood

References

Ackerman, D. (1996). *A slender thread*. New York: Random House.
Addams, Jane (1909). *The spirit of youth and the city streets*. New York: Macmillan.
Ayers, W., & Klonsky, M. (2006). Chicago's Renaissance 2010: The small schools movement meets the ownership society. *Phi Delta Kappan, 87*(6), 453–457.
Bailey, R. (2008). Youth sport and social inclusion. In N.L. Holt (Ed.), *Positive youth development through sport* (pp. 85–96). London: Routledge.
Barry, M. (2005). The inclusive illusion of youth transitions. In M. Barry (Ed.), *Youth policy and social Inclusion: Critical debates with young people* (pp. 97–112). Milton Park, Abingdon: Routledge.
Benson, P.L. (1990). *The case for peers*. Portland, OR: Northwest Educational Regional Laboratory.
Benson, P.L. (1997). *All kids are our kids: What communities must do to raise caring and responsible children and youth*. San Francisco: Jossey-Bass.
Benson, P.L. (2006). (2nd Ed.). *All our kids are your kids: What communities should do to raise caring and responsible children and adolescents*. San Francisco: Jossey-Bass.
Berlin, R.A., Dworkin, A., Earnes, N., Menconi, A., & Perkins, D.F. (2007). Examples of sport-based youth development programs. In D.F. Perkins & S.L. Menestrel (Eds.), *New directions for youth development: Sports-based youth development* (Special Monograph) (pp. 85–108). San Francisco: Jossey-Bass.
Brendtro, L.K., Brokenleg, M., & Van Bockern, S. (2005). The circle of courage and positive psychology. *Reclaiming Children and Youth, 14*, 130–136.
Brown, J. (1979). Description of dyadic student-teacher interaction in physical education class. Unpublished doctoral dissertation, University of North Carolina at Greensboro.
Buchanan, A.M. (1996) Learners' and instructors' interpretations of personal and social responsibility in a sports camp. Unpublished dissertation, Texas A&M University.
Burns, J.M. (1978). *Leadership*. New York: HarperCollins.
Coatsworth, J.D., & Conroy, D.E. (2007). Youth sport as a component of after-school programs. In D.F. Perkins & S.L. Menestrel (Eds.), *New directions for youth development* (Fall), (pp. 13–25). San Francisco: Jossey-Bass.

Coburn, C.E. (2003). Rethinking scale: Moving beyond numbers to deep and lasting change. *Educational Researcher*, 32 (6), 3–12.
Coles, R. (2000). *Lives of moral leadership*. New York: Random House.
Crowe, P. (1983). *Research of teacher expectations*. Paper presented at the annual convention of the American Alliance for Health, Physical Education, Recreation, and Dance. New Orleans, LA.
Cutforth, N. (1997). "What's worth doing": A university professor reflects on an after-school program in a Denver elementary school. *Quest*, 49, 130–139.
Cutforth, N., & Martinek, T. (2000). Cross-age teaching. In D. Hellison, N. Cutforth, J. Kallusky, T. Martinek, M. Parker, & J. Stiehl (Eds.), *Youth development and physical activity* (pp. 172–195). Champaign, IL: Human Kinetics.
Cutforth, N., & Puckett, K. (1999). An investigation into the organization, challenges, and impact of an urban apprentice teacher program. *The Urban Review*, 31(2), 19–23.
Damon, W. (1990). *The moral child: Nurturing children's natural moral growth*. New York: Free Press.
Damon, W. (2008). *The path to purpose: Helping children find their calling in life*. New York: Free Press.
Daniels, A.M. (2007). Cooperation versus competition: Is there really such an issue? In D.F. Perkins & S.L. Menestrel (Eds.), *New directions for youth development*, (Fall), (pp. 13–25). San Francisco: Jossey-Bass.
Debusk, M., & Hellison, D. (1989). Implementing a physical education self responsibility model for delinquency-prone youth. *Journal of Teaching in Physical Education*, 8(2), 104–112.
deCharms, R. (1976). *Enhancing motivation: Change in the classroom*. New York: Irvington.
Demos, E.V. (1989). Resiliency in infancy. In T. Dugan & R. Coles (Eds.), *The child in our times—Studies in the development of resiliency* (pp. 3–22). New York: Bruner/Mazel.
Deschenes, S., McDonald, M., & McLaughlin, M. (2004). Youth organizations: From principles to practice. In S.F. Hamilton & M.A. Hamilton (Eds.), *The youth development handbook* (pp. 25–50). Thousand Oaks, CA: Sage.
Duncan, A. (2006) Chicago's Renaissance 2010: Building on school reform in the age of accountability. *Phi Delta Kappan*, 87(6), 357–458.
Eckerman, C.O., & Didow, S.M. (1988). Lessons drawn from observing young peers together. *Acta Paediatrica Scandinavica*, 77, 55–70.
Eckerman, C.O., Davis, C.C., & Didow, S.M. (1989). Toddlers' emerging ways of achieving social coordination with a peer. *Child Development*, 60, 440–453.
Ennis, C.D., Solomon, M.A., Satina, B., Loftus, S.J., Mensch, J., & McCauley, M.T. (1999). Creating a sense of family in an urban school using the "The sport for peace" curriculum. *Research Quarterly for Exercise and Sport*, 70, 273–285.
Epstein, R. (2007). Why high school must go: An interview with Leon Botstein, *Phi Delta Kappan*, 88(9), 659–663.
Erikson, E. (1988). Real American children: The challenge for after-school programs. *Child and Youth Care Quarterly*, 17(2), 86–103.
Erikson, E. (1994). *Youth: Identity and crisis*. New York: W.W. Norton.

Escarti, A., Pascual, C., & Gutierrez, M. (2005). *Responsibilidad personal social a traves de la education fiscia y el deporte*. Barcelona, Spain: GRAQ.

Fantini, M.D. (Ed.) (1976). *Alternative education: A source book for parents, teachers, students, and administrators*. Garden City, NY: Doubleday.

Fraser-Thomas, Jessica, Cote, J., & Deakin, J. (2005). Youth sport programs: An avenue to foster positive youth development. *Physical Education and Sport Pedagogy*, 10, 19–40.

Friere, P. (1993). *Pedagogy of the oppressed*. New York: Continuum.

Gladwell, M. (2002). *The tipping point: How little things can make a big difference*. New York: Back Bay.

Gilligan, C. (1982). *In a different voice: Psychological theory and women's development*. Cambridge, MA: Harvard University Press.

Ginwright, S., Noguera, P., & Cammarota, J. (2006) (Eds.) *Beyond resistance! Youth: Youth activism and community change*. New York: Routledge.

Goldman, R. (1996). *Disposable children: America's child welfare system*. Belmont, CA: Wadsworth.

Gordon, B. (2005). An evaluation of a six month implementation of the responsibility model in a New Zealand secondary school. Unpublished doctoral dissertation, Massey University College of Education, Palmerston North, New Zealand.

Gould, D., Finch, L.M., & Jackson, S.A. (1993). Coping strategies used by national champion figure skaters. *Research Quarterly for Exercise and Sport*, 64, 453–468.

Greene, M. (1986). Philosophy and teaching. In M.C. Wittrock (Ed.), *The handbook of research on teaching* (3rd Ed.) (pp. 479–504). New York: Macmillan.

Halpern, R. (2003). *Making play work: The promise of after-school programs for low income youth*. New York: Teachers College Press.

Hamilton, S.F., & Hamilton, M.A. (Eds.) (2004). *The youth development handbook*. Thousand Oaks, CA: Sage.

Harris, J. (1998). *The nurture assumption*. New York: Free Press.

Harrison, R., & Wise, C. (2005). *Working with young people*. Thousand Oaks, CA: Sage.

Hartmann, D. (2003). Theorizing sport as social intervention: A view from the grassroots. *Quest*, 55, 118–140.

Hayden, C. (2007). *Children in trouble: The role of families, schools, and communities*. New York: Palgrave Macmillian.

Hellison, D. (1978). *Beyond balls and bats: Alienated (and other) youth in the gym*. Washington, DC: AAHPER.

Hellison, D. (1980). The Magnificent Seven: Inner city wrestlers who won while losing. *The Young Wrestler*, 6, 6–7. Reprinted in: (1982) *Journal of Physical Education, Recreation, and Dance*, 54, 60–61.

Hellison, D. (1983). It only takes one case to prove a possibility…and beyond. In T. Templin & J.K. Olson (Eds.), *Teaching physical education* (pp. 102–106). Champaign, IL: Human Kinetics.

Hellison, D. (1985a). Cause of death: Physical education. *Journal of Physical Education, Recreation, and Dance*, 57, 57–58.

Hellison, D. (1985b). *Goals and strategies for teaching physical education.* Champaign, IL: Human Kinetics.

Hellison, D. (1988). Cause of death: Physical education—A sequel. *Journal of Physical Education, Recreation, and Dance, 59,* 18-2.

Hellison, D. (2003). (2nd Ed.). *Teaching physical education through physical activity.* Champaign, IL: Human Kinetics.

Hellison, D., & Cutforth N. (1997). Extended day programs for urban children and youth: From theory to practice. In H.J. Walberg, O. Reyes, & R.P. Weissberg (Eds.), *Children and youth: Interdisciplinary perspectives* (pp. 223-249). Thousand Oaks, CA: Sage.

Hellison, D., Cutforth, N., Kallusky, J., Martinek, T., Parker, M., & Stiehl, J. (2000). *Youth development and physical activity.* Champaign, IL: Human Kinetics.

Hellison, D., & Martinek, T. (2006). Social and responsibility programs. In D. Kirk, M. O'Sullivan, & D. MacDonald (Eds.), *Handbook of research in physical education* (pp. 610-626). London: Sage.

Hellison, D., Martinek, T., & Walsh, D. (2007). Sport and responsible leadership among youth. In N.L. Holt (Ed.) *Positive youth development and sport* (pp. 49-60). New York: Sage.

Hellison, D., & Walsh, D. (2002). Responsibility-based youth programs evaluation: Investigating the investigations. *Quest, 54,* 292-307.

Hellison, D. & Wright, P. (2003). Retention in an urban extended day program: A process based assessment. *The Journal of Teaching Physical Education, 22,* 369-383.

Heifeitz, R., & Linsky, M. (2002). *Leadership on the line.* Cambridge, MA: Harvard Business School Press.

Hichwa, J. (1998). *Right fielders are people too.* Champaign, IL: Human Kinetics.

Hirsch, B. (2006). *A place to call home—After-school programs for urban youth.* New York: Teachers College Press.

Hodge, K., & Danish, S. (1999). Promoting life skills for males through sport. In A. Horne & M.S. Kiselica (Eds.). *The handbook of counseling boys and adolescent males* (pp. 55-71.). Thousand Oaks, CA: Sage.

Horn, T. (1984). Expectancy effects in the interscholastic athletic setting: Methodological considerations. *Journal of Sport Psychology, 6,* 60-76.

Howe, Q. (1991). *Under running laughter—Note from a renegade classroom.* New York: Free Press—Macmillan.

Intractor, S.M., & Siegel, D. (2008). Project Coach: Youth development and academic achievement through sport. *Journal of Physical Education and Sport,* 79(7), 17-23.

Klau, M., S. Boyd, & L. Luckow (Eds.) (2006). *New directions in youth development youth leadership.* San Francisco: Jossey-Bass.

Klonsky, M., & Klonsky, S. (2008). *Public school reform meets the ownership society.* New York: Routledge.

Kohlberg, H. (1971). Stages of moral development as a basis for moral development. In C.M. Beck, B.S. Crittenden, & E.V. Sullivan (Eds.), *Moral education: Interdisciplinary approaches.* (pp. 234-92). Toronto, Canada: University of Toronto Press.

Kohlberg, L. (1982). *The philosophy of moral development.* New York: HarperCollins.
Kohn, A. (1999). From degrading to de-grading. *High School Magazine,* 6(5), 38–43.
Kohn, A. (2006). (2nd Ed.). *Beyond discipline.* Alexander, VA: Association for Supervision and Curriculum Development.
Komives, S.R., Lucas, T., & McMahon, T.R. (1998). *Exploring leadership: For college students who want to make a difference.* San Francisco: Sage.
Kounin, J. (1970). *Discipline and group management in the classroom.* New York: Holt, Rinehart, & Winston.
Kouzes, J.M., & Posner, B.P. (1987). *The leadership challenge.* San Francisco: Jossey-Bass.
Kouzes, J.M., & Posner, B.Z. (2008). *The student leadership challenge—Five practices for exemplary leaders.* San Francisco: Jossey-Bass.
Kozol, J. (1967). *Death at an early age.* Boston, MA: Houghton Mifflin.
Kozol, J. (1992). Savage inequalities: Children in America's schools. New York: HarperCollins.
Kozol, J. (1995). *Amazing grace.* New York: Crown.
Kozol, J. (2005). *The shame of a nation.* New York: Crown.
Kress, C. (2006). Youth leadership and youth development: Connections and questions. In M. Klau, S. Bolyd, & L. Luckow (Eds.), *New directions for youth development* (pp. 45–56). San Francisco: Jossey-Bass.
Laker, T. (2000). *Beyond the boundaries of physical education: Educating young people for citizenship and social responsibility.* New York: Routledge Falmer.
Langer, E. (1997). *The power of mindful learning.* Reading, MA: Addison-Wesley.
Lawson. H. (1984). Problem-setting for physical education and sport. *Quest,* 36, 48–60.
Lee, O., & Martinek, T. (2009). Navigating two cultures: An investigation of cultures of a responsibility-based physical activity program and school. *Research Quarterly for Exercise and Sport,* 80(2), 41–51.
Lerner, R.M. (2004). *Liberty: Thriving and engagement among America's youth.* Thousand Oaks, CA: Sage.
Lerner, R.M., Taylor, C.S., & von Eye, A. (Eds.) (2002). *New directions for youth development—Pathways to positive development among diverse youth.* San Francisco: Jossey-Bass.
Li, W., Wright, P.M., Rukavina, P.B., & Pickering, M. (2008). Measuring students' perceptions of personal and social responsibility and the relationship to intrinsic motivation in urban physical education. *Journal of teaching in physical education,* 27, 167–178.
Libby, M., Sedonaen, M., & Bliss, S. (2006). The mystery of youth leadership development: The path to just communities. In M. Klau, S. Boyd, & L. Luckow (Eds.) *New directions: Theory into practice* (pp. 13–25). San Francisco: Jossey-Bass.
Libby, M., Sedonaen, &, Bliss, S. (2006). The mystery of youth leadership development: The path to just communities. In M. Klau, S. Bolyd, & L. Luckow

(Eds.), *New directions for youth development* (pp. 13–25). San Francisco: Jossey-Bass.

Lincoln, Y.S., & Guba, E.G. (1985). *Naturalistic inquiry*. Thousand Oaks, CA: Sage.

Littky, D. (2004). *The big picture—Education is everyone's business*. Alexandria, VA: Association for Supervision and Curriculum Development.

Lytle, J.H. (2002). Whole-school freeform from the inside. *Phi Delta Kappan*, 84 (2), 164–167.

Mandigo, J., Corlett, J., & Anderson, A. (2008). Using quality physical education to promote positive youth development in a developing nation. In N.L. Holt (Ed.) *Positive youth development through sport* (pp. 110–121). London: Routledge.

Markus, H., & Nurius, P. (1986). Possible selves. *American Psychologist*, 41, 954–969.

Martinek, T. (1981) Pygmalion in the gym: A model for the communication of teacher expectations in physical education. *Research Quarterly for Exercise and Sport*, 52, 58–67.

Martinek, T. (1983). Creating "Golem" and "Galatea" effects in physical education instruction. In T. Templin & J. Olson (Eds.), *Teaching in physical education* (pp. 59–70). Champaign, IL: Human Kinetics Publishers.

Martinek, T. (l989a). Children's perceptions of teaching behaviors: An attributional model for explaining teacher expectancy effects. *Journal of Teaching in Physical Education*, 4, 318–328.

Martinek, T. (l989b). Psycho-social dynamics of the Pygmalion phenomenon in physical education. In Templin & Schempp (Eds.) *Socialization into physical education: Learning to teach*. Indianapolis, IN: Benchmark Press.

Martinek, T. (1997). *Psycho-social dynamics of teaching physical education*. (Dubuque, IA: Brown & Benchmark.

Martinek, T. (2000). Program evaluation. In Hellison, D., Cutforth, N., Kallusky, J. Martinek, T., Parker, M., Stiehl, J. (Eds.) *Youth development and physical activity* (pp. 211–228), Champaign, IL: Human Kinetics.

Martinek, T., & Griffith, J.B. (1993). Working with the learned helpless child: *Journal of Physical Education, Recreation, and Dance*, 64, 17–20.

Martinek, T., & Hellison, D. (1997). Service-bonded inquiry: The road less traveled. *The Journal of Teaching Physical Education*, 17, 107–121.

Martinek, T., Hellison, D., & Walsh, D. (2004). Service-bonded inquiry revisited: A research model for the community-engaged professor, *Quest*, 56, 397–412.

Martinek, T., & Karper, W. (1986). Motor ability and instructional contexts: Effects on teacher expectation and dyadic interactions in elementary physical education classes. *Journal of Classroom Interaction*, 21(2), 16–25.

Martinek, T., McLaughlin, D., & Schilling, T. (1999). Project effort: Teaching responsibility beyond the gym. *Journal Physical Education, Recreation, and Dance*, 70, 12–25.

Martinek, T., & Ruiz, L.M. (2005). Promoting positive youth development through a values-based sport program. *International Journal of Sport Science*, 1(1), 1–13.

Martinek, T., & Schilling, T. (2003). Developing compassionate leadership in underserved youth. *Journal of Physical Education, Recreation, and Dance*, 74, 33–39.

Martinek, T., Schilling, T., & Hellison, D. (2006). The development of compassionate and caring leadership among adolescent youth. *Physical Education and Sport Pedagogy*, 11(2), 141–157.

Martinek, T., Schilling, T., & Johnson, D. (1999). Evaluation of a sport and mentoring program designed to foster personal and social responsibility in underserved youth. *Urban Review*, 33, 29–45.

Martinek, T., Hellison, D., & Walsh, D. (2004). Service-bonded inquiry revisited: A research model for the community-engaged professor. *Quest*, 56, 397–412.

Martinek, T., Schilling, T., & Hellison, D. (2006). The development of compassionate and caring leadership among adolescents. *Physical Education and Sport Pedagogy*. 11(2), 141–157.

Martinek, T., Schilling, T., & Johnson, D. (2001). Evaluation of a sport and mentoring program designed to foster personal and social responsibility in underserved youth. *The Urban Review*, 33, 29–45.

Matsudaira, J. & Jefferson, A. (2006). Anytown: NCCJ's youth leadership experience in social justice. In M. Klau, S. Boyd, & L. Luckow (Eds.) *New directions for youth development—Youth Leadership* (pp. 107–115), San Francisco: Jossey-Bass.

McDonald, J.P. (1992). *Teaching: Making sense of an uncertain craft*. New York: Teachers College Press.

McDonald, D., Kirk, D., Metzler, M., Nilges, L.M., Schempp, P., & Wright, J. (2002). It's all very well, in theory: Theoretical considerations and practical implications in contemporary pedagogy. *Quest*, 54, 133–156.

McLaughlin, M.W. (2000). *Community counts*. Washington, DC: Public Education Network.

McLaughlin, M. & Heath, S. (1993). Casting the self: Frames for identity and dilemmas for policy. In S. Heath & McLaughlin, M (Eds.) *Identity and inner city youth: Beyond ethnicity and gender* (pp. 210–239). New York: Teacher College Press.

McLaughlin, M.W., Irby, M.A., & Langman, J. (1994). *Urban sanctuaries: Neighborhood organizations in the lives and futures of inner-city youth*. San Francisco: Jossey-Bass.

Menestrel, S.E., & Perkins, D.F. (2007). Overview of how sports, out-of-school time, and youth well-being can and do intersect. In D.F. Perkins & S.L. Menestrel (Eds.), *New Directions for youth development (Fall)*, (pp. 13–25). San Francisco: Jossey-Bass.

Mohamed, I., & Wheeler, W. (2001). *Broadening the bounds of youth development: Youth as engaged citizens*. Chevy Chase, MD: Innovation Center and Ford Foundation.

Mosston, M., & Ashworth, S. (1994). *Teaching physical education*. 4th Ed. New York: Macmillan.

Mrugala, J. (2002). *Explorative study of responsibility* and *practitioners*. Ph.D. dissertation, University of Illinois at Chicago.

Myrdal, G. (1944). *An American dilemma: The Negro problem and modern democracy.* New York: Harper.
National Research Council & Institute of Medicine (2002). *Community programs to promote youth development.* Washington, DC: National Academy Press.
Noam, G.G., Biancarosa, G., & Dechausay, N. (2003). *Afterschool education: Approaches to an emerging field.* Cambridge, MA: Harvard University Press.
Noddings, N. (1992). *The challenge to care in schools.* New York: Teachers College Press.
North Carolina Employment Security Commission Report (2007). *Annual publication of job status Guilford County from the Greenboro Employment Security Commission.* Greensboro North Carolina.
Orlick, T. (1980). *In pursuit of excellence.* Champaign, IL: Human Kinetics.
O'Sullivan, R. (1993). *Programs for at-risk youth—A guide to evaluation.* Newbury Park, CA: Sage.
Patton, M. (1989). *Creative evaluation.* Newbury Park, CA: Sage.
Perkins, D.F., & Menestrel, S.L. (Eds.) (Fall 2007). *New directions for youth development.* San Francisco: Jossey-Bass.
Perkins, D.F., & Noam, G.G, (2007). Characteristics of sports-based youth development programs. In D.F. Perkins & S.L. Menestrel (Eds.), *New Directions for youth development,* (Fall), (pp. 75–84). San Francisco: Jossey-Bass.
Petitpas, A.J., Cornelius, A.E., Van Raalte, J.L., & Jones, T. (2005). A framework for planning youth sport programs that foster psychosocial development. *The Sport Psychologist, 19,* 63–80.
Phelan, P. K., Davidson, A.L., & Yu, H. C. (1998). *Adolescents' worlds: Negotiating family, peers and school.* New York: Teachers College Press.
Power, F.C. (2002).Building democratic community: A radical approach to moral education. In W. Damon (Ed.) *Bringing a new era in character education* (129–148). Palo Alto, CA: Hoover Institute Press.
Prather, H. (1970). *Notes to myself: My struggle to become a person.* Mooab, UT: Real Person Press.
Project Effort (2000). Trying in the Classroom Inventory. Unpublished document, University of North Carolina at Greensboro.
Putnam, R. (2000). *Bowling alone: The collapse and revival of American community.* New York: Simon & Schuster.
Raywid, M.A. (1994). Alternative schools. The state of the art. *Educational Leadership, 52,* 26–31.
Reguieras, L. (2008). Leaders' voices in youth development. Unpublished research report. University of Oporto, Portugal.
Rhodes, J.E. (2004). The critical ingredient: caring youth-staff relationships in after school settings. *New Directions for Youth Development,* No. 101, 145–161. San Francisco: Jossey-Bass.
Richards, A. (1982). Seeking roots from Hahn. *Journal for Experiential Education, 5,* 22–25.
Rodriguez, L. (2001). *Hearts and hands: Creating community in violent times.* New York: Seven Stories Press.

Rogers, P.A., Hacsi, T.A., Petrosino, A., & Huebner, T.A. (Eds.) (2000). *Program theory in evaluation: Challenges and opportunities*. San Francisco, CA: Jossey-Bass.
Rosenthal, R., & Jacobson, L. (1968). *Pygmalion in the classroom: Teacher expectation and pupils intellectual development*. New York: Holt, Rinehart, & Winston.
Rothstein, R. (2004). *Class and schools: Social, economic, and educational reform to close the black-white achievement gap*. New York: Economic Policy Institute.
Rovegno, I. and Kirk, D. (1995). Articulations and silences in socially critical work on physical education.: Toward a broader agenda. *Quest*, 47, 447–474.
Rubin, L. (1985). *Artistry in teaching*. New York: Random House.
Ruffini, J.P. (1980). *Disciple: Negotiating conflict with today's kids*. Englewood Cliffs, NJ: Prentice-Hall.
Sandford, R.A., Armour, K.M., & Duncombe, R. (2008). Physical activity and personal/social development for disaffected youth in the UK. In N.L. Holt, *Positive youth development through sport* (pp. 97–109). London: Routledge.
Scales, P.C., & Roehlkepartain, E.C. (2004). *Community service and service learning in U.S. public schools, 2004: Findings from a national survey*. St. Paul, MN: National Leadership Council.
Schilling, T. (1999). An investigation of commitment among participants in an extended-day physical activity program. Unpublished doctoral dissertation. University of North Carolina at Greensboro.
Schilling, T. (2001). An investigation of commitment among participants in an extended-day physical activity program. *Research Quarterly for Exercise and Sport*. 72(4), 355–365.
Schilling, T. (2008). An examination of residence processes in context: The case of Tasha. *Urban Review*, 40, 296–316.
Schilling, T., Martinek, T., & Carson, S. (2007). Developmental processes among youth leaders in an after-school, responsibility-based sport program: Antecedents and barriers to commitment. *Research Quarterly for Exercise and Sport*. 78, 48–60.
Schilling, T. Martinek, T., & Tan, C. (2001). Fostering youth development through power sharing. In B.J. Loindardo, T.J. Caravella-Nadeau, H.S. Castagno & V.H. Mancini (Eds.) *Sport in the Twenty-first Century—Alternative for the New Millennium* (pp. 169–180), Boston: Pearson.
Schine, J. (Ed.) (1997). *Service learning*. Chicago: University of Chicago Press.
Schon, D.A. (1987). *Educating the reflective practitioner*. San Francisco. Jossey-Bass.
Scriven, M. (1997). The vision thing: Educational research and AERA in the 21st century—Part 1: Competing visions of what educational researchers should do. *Educational Researcher*, 20(4), 18.
Seligson, M., & Stahl, P. (2003). *Bringing yourself to work: A guide to successful staff development in after-school programs*. New York: Teachers College Press.

Sherrod, L. (2006). Promoting citizenship and activism in today's youth. In S. Ginwright, P. Noguera, & J. Cammarota (Eds.) *Beyond resistance! Youth activism and community change* (pp. 287–299). New York: Routledge.

Shields, D., & Bredemeier, B. (1995). *Character development and physical activity.* Champaign, IL: Human Kinetics.

Siedentop, D. (1990). *Introduction to physical education, fitness, and sport.* Mountain View, CA: Mayfield.

Siedentop, D. (1994). *Sport education: Quality PE through positive sport experiences.* Champaign, IL.: Human Kinetics.

Siedentop, D. (1998). *Sport education.* Champaign, IL: Human Kinetics.

Swinehart, B. (1990). *Youth involvement: Developing leaders and strengthening communities.* Boulder, CO: Partners for Youth Leadership.

Strengthening the youth work profession (1996). New York: DeWitt Wallace-Readers Digest Fund.

Thompson, N. (2005). Anti-discriminatory practices. In R. Harrison and C. Wise (Eds.) *Working with young people* (pp. 166–175). Thousand Oaks, CA: Sage.

Tom, A. (1984). *Teaching as a moral craft.* New York: Longman.

Tribe, C. (2008). *Sport 37.* Chicago, IL.: Chicago Park District.

Turner, M. (2007). Investigating student leadership in senior high school physical education. Unpublished Master's thesis, University of Otago, Dunnedin, New Zealand.

United Way of Greater Greensboro (2001). Summary of program outcome model. Unpublished document from the United Way of Greensboro.

Van Linden, J.A., & Fertman, C.I. (1998). *Youth leadership—A guide to understanding leadership development in adolescents.* San Francisco: Jossey-Bass.

Van Tulder, M., Van der Vegt, R., Veenman, S. (1993). In-service education in innovating schools: A Multi-case study. *Qualitative Studies in Education*, 6(2), 129–142.

Vizzo, C.V., Connell, J.P., Gambone, M.A., & Bradshaw, C.P. (2004). In S.F. Hamilton & M.A. Hamilton (Eds.). *The youth development handbook* (pp. 301–326). Thousand Oaks, CA: Sage.

Walsh, D. (2002). Emerging strategies in the search for effective university-community Collaboration. *Journal of Physical Education, Recreation, and Dance*, 73(1), 50–53.

Walsh, D. (2008). Helping youth in underserved communities envision possible futures: An extension of the teaching personal and social responsibility model. *Research Quarterly for Exercise and Sport*, 79(2), 208–201.

Wang, M.C. & Gordon, E.W. (Eds.) (1994). *Educational residence in inner-city America.* Hillsdale, NJ: Lawrence Erlbaum.

Watson, D. L., Newton, M., & Kim, Mi-Sook (2003). Recognition of values-based constructs in a summer physical activity program. *Urban Review*, 35, 221–232.

Wenger, E. (2005). A social theory of learning. In R. Harrison & C. Wise (Eds.) *Working with young people* (pp. 142–149). Thousand Oaks, CA: Sage.

Wentzel, K.R. (1991). Social competence at school: Relation between social responsibility and academic achievement. *Review of Educational Research*, 61, 1–24.

Witt, P.A., & Crompton, J.L. (2002). *Best practices in youth development in public park and recreation settings*. Ashburn, PA: National Recreation and Park Association.

Wright, P.M. & White, K. (2004). Exploring the relevance of the personal and social responsibility model in adapted physical activity: A collective case study. *Journal of Teaching in Physical Education*, 23, 71–87.

Wright, P.M., White, K., & Gaebler-Spira, D. (2004). Exploring the relevance of the personal and social responsibility model in adapted physical activity: A collective case study, *Journal of Teaching in Physical Education*, 23, 71–87.

Zander, R.S., & Zander, B. (2000). *The art of possibility*. Boston: Harvard.

Index

Ackerman, Diane, 8
acknowledgments, xix
acronyms, use of, 67
adult leader, 103–104
adult leader, personal attributes of
  cultural awareness, 107
  genuineness, 106
  intuition, 106–107
  relational time, 107–108
adult leader, problems for
  building a TPSR foundation, 114–115
  unique program variables, 115–120
  youth leader issues, 120–122
Americorps, 166
Apprentice Teachers Program, 141, 161
assessment
  crosswalk, 149–150
  formative, 137–138
  of the adult leader, 145–146
  of the program, 146–150
  of the youth leader, 139–145
  summative, 138
  use of comparison groups, 150–151

Baldwin, Stephanie, 166
Berg, Kim, 78, 167
Beyond the Ball, 24, 25
Bill and Melinda Gates Foundation, 128
Black Business Owners Association, 98
Botstein, Leon, 4
Boys and Girls Club, 3, 25, 27, 78, 95, 115, 166, 167
Breakfast Club, 78, 167
Brown vs. the Topeka School Board, 31
Burns, Jerome, 9

Campion, Nancy Leader, 3
Career Club, 45, 75, 92–94
Castaneda, Amy and Rob, 24
challenges to becoming leaders
  becoming intrinsically motivated, 10
  leading without controlling, 10
  personal life events, 10
  rebuffing peer pressure, 9
chapters overview, xv-xvii
Chicago Workforce Development Partnership, 92
citizenship, definition of, 33
citizenship, elements of
  moral and social responsibility, 34
  community involvement, 34
  political literacy, 34–35
  activism, 35
"club" concept, 5, 62
club program format, example of, 6
Columbine tragedy, 29
Crabbe, Tim, 52

cross-age leadership, 75–87
cross-age leadership, approaches to
  assisting in a lesson, 77
  teaching a large and small
    group, 77
cross-age leadership, success of
  celebration, 86–87
  community connections, 77–79
  opportunities to lead, 82–84
  orientation and training, 80–82
  program routine, 79–80
  reflection, 84–86
Cutforth, Nick, 44, 75, 85, 86, 92, 106, 167

Damon, William, 65, 169
Doolittle, Sarah, 107
Durham, George, 98
Dworkin, Aaron, xv, 24

El Salvador, 132, 133
Energizer Club, 75, 167
Erikson, Erik, 90
Escarti, Amparo, 159

first person, use of, xiv
First Tee, 19
Forsberg, Nick, 62, 103, 176
four B's of leadership, 81, 180

Gallery 37, 22
Gammage, Phillip, 137
Gandhi, Mahatma, 169
Garcia, Stein, 45
Going for the Goal, 20

Habitat for Humanity, 76
Hahn, Kurt, 174
Halpern, Robert, 22
Harlem RBI, 21
Harris, Eric, 29
Harris, Judith, 12
Hellison, Don
  celebrations, 86
  clubs, 5–7

community service, 94
preface, xiii–xvii
Hichwa, John, 130
Hirsch, Barton, 9
Hollins, James, 167
Hoops and Leaders Basketball
  Camp, xv, 21, 24
Horrocks, Bob, 44
Horton, Myles, 169
Howard, Ken, 165
Howe, Quincy, 11

identity formation, 90
in-school physical education
  in other countries, 130–132
  influence of school size and
    purpose, 127–129
  issues, 125–126
  institutions of higher
    learning, 92
inclusion, definition of, 28
intrinsic vs. extrinsic rewards, 174
intuition, definition of, 106

Jones, Ricky Lee, 65

Kallusky, James, 170
Kelly, Walt, 177
Kleibold, Dillon, 29
Kohn, Alfie, 83, 145
Kounin, Jacob, 81

leadership, alternative conception
  of, 4
leadership awareness
  acknowledging leadership, 66
  peer and team coaching, 66–73
leadership development
  role of physical activity, 8–9
  stages of, 42–45
leadership opportunities
  categories, 4
leadership program, starting beliefs
  about kids, 11–12
leadership roles, negative, 3

leadership, self-actualized
  adult roles, 97–99
  sources of support
    career clubs, 92–94
    community service, 94–95
    institutions of higher learning, 91–92
    internship programs, 95–97
learned helplessness, 162
Littky, Dennis, 48
Living for Sport, 131

Macha, Nsandjo, 166
Martin, Pedro, 159
Martinek, Tom
  preface, xiii–xvii
  celebrations, 86
  clubs, 5–7
  community service, 95
McDonald, Joe, 113
McLaughlin, Dan, 44
Midnight Basketball, 32
moral development theories, 162

National Association of Sport and Physical Education, 16, 126
National Federation of High Schools, 16
National Youth Sport Program (NYSP), 5, 94
Neighborhood Scholar Program, 92
New Zealand, xv, 52, 130–131, 133, 154, 159
Nike, 92
No Child Left Behind, 117, 158, 167

Obama, Barack, 27
Outward Bound, 174

peer coaching, 66–69
Percy, Walter, 3
personal and social responsibility levels, 6
Petitpas, Al, 19; foreword, xi–xii

Play It Smart, 19, 20
Portugal, 52, 154
pre-post program reflection, 121
problem-solving vignettes, 108–111
problem-setting, 113
program commitment, 149, 156, 162
program variables, 115
Program Outcome Model, 148–150
Project Coach, xv, 23–24
Project Effort Sport Club, 5, 62, 89, 90, 144, 156–159, 162

Quality Physical Education (QPE), 132
question-answer ratio, 57

reasons for leading others, 162
Reeder, Mike, 66
reflection-in-action, 106, 109
reflection-in-action vs. knowing-in-action, 60, 120
Reguieras, Leonor, 159–160
relationships with leaders, 103–111
  director-youth leader relationship qualities, 104–108
  relational problem-solving vignettes, 108–111
Right Fielders Are People Too, 130, 133

scapegoating, social and individual, 32
Schilling, Tammy, 144, 156–158, 161–163
Scriven, Michael, 138
selection of teams, 70–71
self-fulfilling expectations, 31
servant leadership, 174
service-bonded inquiry, 154, 163, 175
service learning, 76
Siedentop, Daryl, 70, 130, 131
skillful inaction, 107
Snowsports Outreach Society, 21

social injustice, 27–33
 exclusion and unfairness, 28–30
 stereotyping and expectations, 30–31
 stigmatization, 31–33
solutions bank, 59–60, 106
South Africa, 52
Spain, 52, 154, 159
Sport and physical education
 professional preparation for, 16–17
sport court, 60
Sport for Peace, 131, 133
Sports 37, xiv, 22–23, 176
stereotyping and expectations, 30–31
Stewart, Craig, 16
Summer Apprentice Teaching Program, 92

Taking/Teaching Personal and Social Responsibility (TPSR) model, xi, xiii, 3, 51–63
 adult leader responsibilities, 60–62
 pay back of, 3
 primer, 139
 program format, 56–59
 purpose of, 52
 research
  individual program studies, 155–159
  international studies, 159–160
 strategies for problems that arise, 59–60
 student responsibilities, 53–56
 youth leadership program studies, 160–163
task card, 67–68
teaching for transfer, 61
team coaching, 69–73
ten-word rule, 57, 115
theory of possible selves, 92

Title IX legislation, and expectancy research, 31
Tom, Alan, 113
TPSR, 51–53
training programs, 80–81
transformational process, 9
Tribe, Charlie, xiv, 22, 176
Trying in the Classroom Inventory, 143–144
Turner, Murray, xv, 130
Twine, Judy, 68
Tzu, Lao, 41

United Kingdom, 131, 133
United Way, 149
University of Porto, 159
University of Regina, 176
Urban Youth Leader Project, 5, 75

Vulnerability, 106

Walsh, Dave, 44, 45, 71, 75, 78, 92
with-it-ness, 81
Wright, Paul, 155,156

youth development
 emergence of, 17–19
 sport-based, 19–21
Youth Leader Corps, 5, 32, 75, 80–81, 89, 92, 96, 145, 162–163, 168
youth leadership
 and in-school physical education, 126
 impact on youth leaders, 162–163
 in sport and physical education, 21–22
 issues, 7
 problem solving in, 113–123
 sport-based programs, 22–25
 sustained involvement in, 162

youth leadership approach, 173–174
youth leadership development
  importance of, 7–8
  lack of, 8
youth leadership development, stages of
  cross-age leadership, 44–45, 75–87
  leadership awareness, 43–44, 65–74
  learning to take responsibility, 43, 51–63
  self-actualized leadership, 45, 89–100
youth leadership development, themes for advancement
  integration, 49
  power sharing, 46–47
  relationships, 48–49
  self-reflection, 47–48
  transfer, 49
youth leadership program, strategies for starting
  connecting with resources, 167–169
  maintaining your values, 171
  preparing for challenges, 169–171
  starting small, 166–167
Youth Sport Trust, 131

GPSR Compliance
The European Union's (EU) General Product Safety Regulation (GPSR) is a set of rules that requires consumer products to be safe and our obligations to ensure this.

If you have any concerns about our products, you can contact us on

ProductSafety@springernature.com

In case Publisher is established outside the EU, the EU authorized representative is:

Springer Nature Customer Service Center GmbH
Europaplatz 3
69115 Heidelberg, Germany

www.ingramcontent.com/pod-product-compliance
Lightning Source LLC
LaVergne TN
LVHW011819060526
838200LV00053B/3838

9 781349 377206